HISTORY DETECTIVES

Science and Technology

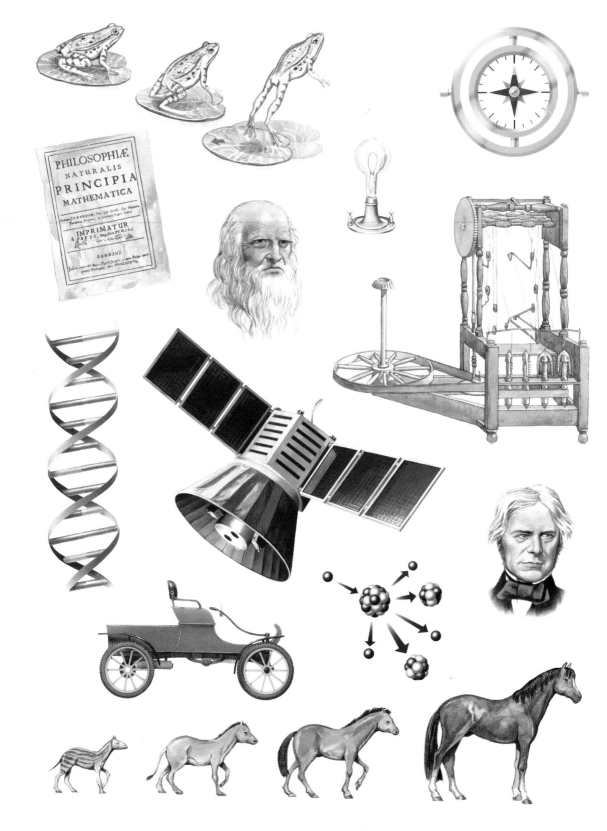

HISTORY DETECTIVES

Science and Technology

The amazing story of inventions and discoveries

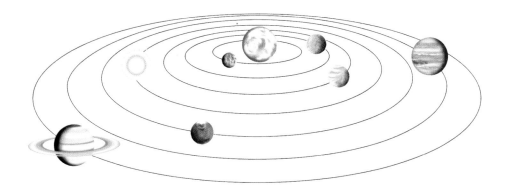

John Farndon

southwater

This edition is published by Southwater

Southwater is an imprint of Anness Publishing Ltd
Hermes House, 88–89 Blackfriars Road, London SE1 8HA
tel. 020 7401 2077; fax 020 7633 9499
www.southwaterbooks.com; info@anness.com
© Anness Publishing Ltd 2000, 2003

UK agent: The Manning Partnership Ltd
tel. 01225 478 444; fax 01225 478 440; sales@manning-partnership.co.uk

UK distributor: Grantham Book Services Ltd
tel. 01476 541080; fax 01476 541061; orders@gbs.tbs-ltd.co.uk

North American agent/distributor: National Book Network
tel. 301 459 3366; fax 301 429 5746; www.nbnbooks.com

Australian agent/distributor: Pan Macmillan Australia
tel. 1300 135 113; fax 1300 135 103; customer.service@macmillan.com.au

Publisher: Joanna Lorenz
Managing Editor: Gilly Cameron Cooper
Senior Editor: Lisa Miles

Produced by Miles Kelly Publishing Limited
The Bardfield Centre,
Great Bardfield, Essex CM7 4SL

Publishing Director: Jim Miles
Editorial Director: Paula Borton
Art Director: Clare Sleven
Project Editors: Neil de Cort, Cindy Leaney
Assistant Editors: Simon Nevill, Helen Parker
Design: Angela Ashton
Art Commissioning: Susanne Grant, Lynne French
Picture Research: Kate Miles, Janice Bracken
Lesley Cartlidge, Liberty Mella

The publishers would like to thank the following
artists who have contributed to this book:
Richard Hook (Linden Artists); John James (Temple Rogers);
Terry Riley Studio; Martin Sanders; Peter Sarson; Rob Sheffield;
Mike White (Temple Rogers); Kuo Chen Kang; Rob Jakeway;
Chris Forsey; Jeremy Gower; Janos Marffy; Nick Spender (Advocate); Andrew
Robinson; Mike Foster (Malting Partnership).

The publishers wish to thank the following
for supplying photographs for this book:
Page 10 (C/R) Ann Ronan; 11 (B/L) Image Select; 17 (C/R) Corbis; 18 (C)
Corbis; 19 (T/R, B/L) Ann Ronan; 20 (T/R) Mary Evans; 21 (C/R) Image Select;
21 (B/L) NASA; 23 (C/L) NASA; 24 (T/R) Ann Ronan; 24 (B/R) Corbis; 25
(B/L) Corbis; 26 (B/L, B/R) Ann Ronan; 29 (T/R) American Institute of Physics;
29 (B/L) Mary Evans; 30 (B/R, B/C) Ann Ronan; 33 (T/R) Mary Evans; 35
(C/R) Ford Motor Company; 36 (B/R) Virgin Atlantic Airways Limited; 37 (C)
Corbis; 38 (T/R) Science Photo Library; 39 (T/R) Corbis; 40 (T/R, B/L) Corbis;
40 (T/L, T/R) Corbis; 41 (T/R) Richard Morrell/ Science Photo Library; 44
(C/R) Corbis; 45 (T/R) Mary Evans; 45 (B/L) Geoff Tompkinson/Science Photo
Library; 46 (B/C) Corbis; 49 (B/L) Tek Image/Science Photo Library; 50 (C/R)
Firefly Productions/Science Photo Library; 50 (B/L) American Institute of
Physics; 51 (C/R) Sony Computer Entertainment (U.K.); 51 (C)
Reproduced by kind permission of Apple Computer U.K. Limited; 53 (B/L)
NASA; 56 (T/R) Naoto Hosaka/ Frank Spooner Pictures; 56 (B/R) Adam G.
Sylvester/Science Photo Library; 57 (B/C) Frank Spooner Pictures; 59 (T/C)
Allsport at Image Select; 59 (B/L) Science Photo Library; 60 (B/C) R.
Benali/S.Ferry/Frank Spooner Pictures; 61 (B/L) Corbis.

All other photographs from Miles Kelly archives.

Previously Published as Exploring History: Science and Technology

1 3 5 7 9 10 8 6 4 2

CONTENTS

Introduction
6

Inventing
Mathematics
8

Star Gazing
10

The First
Scientist
12

Roman Engineers
14

Where and When
16

The Great
Anatomists
18

The Moving Earth
20

Force and
Motion
22

Atoms
and Matter
24

Factory and
Furnace
26

The Charged
World
28

Steam Power
30

The Story
of Life
32

On the Road
34

Off the Ground
36

Rays and
Radiation
38

Space and Time
40

The Big
Universe
42

Miracle Cures
44

Nuclear Power
46

Lifeplan
48

The Power of
the Processor
50

Space Age
52

Instant Contact
54

The Moving
Earth
56

Artificial Materials
58

Life Changing
60

Glossary
62

Index
64

Introduction

▲ PYTHAGORAS
Great thinkers such as Pythagoras of Samos (560–480B.C.) are essential to scientific progress. Without the input of people like Pythagoras, Albert Einstein and Louis Pasteur there would be no scientific advances at all.

▼ KEY DATES
This panel charts the progress of science through the ages, from the invention of the wheel to the creation of the World Wide Web.

SCIENCE AND TECHNOLOGY SEEM VERY modern ideas, but humans have been striving to understand the world and inventing machines to help them ever since they first walked on the Earth 30,000 years ago.

The earliest people lived simply by hunting animals and gathering fruit, and there was no need for science to be anything but basic. But as people settled down to farm, around 10,000 years ago, the first towns and cities were built in the Middle East, and life became much more complicated. At once science and technology began to develop apace to meet their varied needs. The Babylonians, for instance, created numbers and mathematics to keep track of goods and taxes. The Egyptians studied astronomy to help them make a calendar. And the astonishing achievements of Greek thinkers like Archimedes and the engineers of the Roman Empire laid the foundations of modern science and technology.

Their achievements were almost lost with the collapse of the Roman Empire, which plunged Europe

▼ OVERCOMING PROBLEMS
Most of the great explorers had used square-sailed ships, which were limited in their manoeuvrability. The development of new technology, such as this caravel with its triangular sails which could sail almost directly into the wind, opened up new possibilities.

EUROPE

c.3200B.C. The wheel is invented in Sumeria.

c.2500B.C. The ancient Egyptians devise a 365-day calendar.

c.1500B.C. The Babylonians develop numbers.

c.300B.C. Euclid writes *Elements of Geometry*.

c.250B.C. Archimedes establishes the mathematical rules for levers.

221–206B.C. The Great Wall of China is built.

A.D.130 Galen writes his medical books.

140 Ptolemy writes *Almagest*.

c.850 Al-Kharwarizmi introduces algebra.

1492 Christopher Columbus sails across the Atlantic.

1543 Copernicus shows that the Earth circles the Sun.

1610 Galileo spies Jupiter's moons through a telescope

1628 Harvey shows how the heart circulates blood.

1661 Boyle introduces the idea of chemical elements and compounds.

1686 Newton establishes his three laws of motion and his theory of gravity.

1698 Savery invents the first practical steam engine.

1735 Linnaeus groups plants into species and genera.

1752 Franklin shows that lightning is electricity.

1783 The Montgolfier brothers' balloon carries two men aloft.

1789 Lavoisier writes the first list of elements.

1804 Trevithick builds the first steam locomotive.

1808 Dalton proposes his atomic theory of chemical elements.

1830 Faraday and Henry find that electricity can be generated by magnetism.

1825 The first passenger railroad, from Stockton to Darlington, in England.

▲ FIRST CARS
The invention of the automobile has had a huge impact on transport throughout the world. The slow and noisy early cars have been replaced by quieter, safer and more economical models. Prices have come down, and the range of makes is now greater than ever. The car has, in fact, been so successful that many countries are now trying to limit car ownership because of the impact on the environment.

into the Dark Ages. But scientific thought continued to flourish in the Islamic east and farther east in China. And as eastern ideas gradually filtered into Europe in the 15th century, European scholars began to rediscover Greek and Roman science and make new discoveries of their own.

The next 100 years brought great shocks to established ideas. First, in 1492, Columbus sailed across the Atlantic to discover a whole new, undreamed-of land. Then, in 1543, Copernicus showed that the Earth, far from being the center of the Universe, was just one of the planets circling around the Sun.

Deep thinkers realized that ancient ideas could not necessarily be trusted: the only way to learn the truth was to look and learn for themselves. Observation and experiment became the basis of a new approach to science which has led to a huge range of discoveries such as Newton's laws of motion, Dalton's atoms, Darwin's theory of the evolution of life, and many more—right up to recent breakthroughs in the science of genetics. Trade and industry, meanwhile, have fueled a revolution in technology, which began with the steam-powered factory machines of the late 18th century and continues to gather pace with the latest computer technology of today.

▼ MIR
Despite a number of mishaps, the Soviet Mir spacecraft stayed up in space for over 13 years, between 1986 and 1999, and made more than 76,000 orbits of the Earth. It was a temporary home to many astronauts—and Russian Valery Polyakov spent a record 437 continuous days aboard.

1856 Mendel discovers the basic laws of heredity.

1858 Darwin and Wallace suggest the theory of evolution by natural selection.

1861 Pasteur shows that many diseases are caused by germs.

1862 Lenoir builds the first internal combustion engine car.

1862 Maxwell proposes that light is electromagnetic radiation.

1876 Alexander Graham Bell sends the first telephone message.

1888 Hertz discovers radio waves.

1895 Rontgen discovers X-rays.

1897 Thomson discovers electrons, and Becquerel discovers radioactivity.

1898 Marie and Pierre Curie discover the radioactive elements radium and polonium.

1900 Planck suggests quantum theory.

1903 Orville and Wilbur Wright make the first controlled, powered flight.

1905 & 1915 Einstein's special and general theories of relativity.

1908 Ford's Model T, the first mass-produced car.

1911 Rutherford shows that atom has a nucleus circled by electrons.

1923 Wegener suggests continental drift.

1927-9 Hubble realizes that there are other galaxies and that the universe is expanding.

1928 Fleming discovers penicillin.

1935 Carothers develops nylon.

1939 Hahn and Strassman split a uranium atom.

1945 The USAF drops atomic bombs on Nagasaki and Hiroshima.

1948 Shockley, Bardeen, and Brattain invent the transistor.

1953 Crick and Watson show that DNA, the gene molecule in living cells, has a double-spiral shape.

1957 Sputnik is the first spacecraft to orbit the Earth.

1969 Armstrong and Aldrin are the first men on the Moon.

1989 Berners-Lee creates the World Wide Web.

Inventing Mathematics

▲ CUNEIFORM
The first writing came hand in hand with the development of numbers. This is Sumerian cuneiform (wedge-form) writing.

PEOPLE PROBABLY LEARNED TO count using numbers many, many thousands of years ago. In fact, even small animals have a basic number sense. Birds usually know how many babies they have, for example. However, it was only when primitive hunters began to settle down and farm, around 10,000 years ago, that people started to think in terms of larger numbers. Then, for the first time, people needed to count things properly. They needed to count how many sheep they were selling at the market, how many bags of wheat they were buying, and so on. So the first farms and the first towns appeared in the Middle East, together with the first numbers, in the ancient civilizations of people such as the Sumerians.

People probably started by counting on fingers. This idea worked well, as it still does today, but fingers do not help you to remember how many. So people began to make the first number records by dropping stones, shells, or clay disks one by one into a bag. In Sumeria, about 6,000 years ago, someone had the bright idea of making scratch marks on a clay tablet—one mark for each thing they were counting. Soon the Babylonians learned to use different-shaped marks for larger numbers. This system is still the basis of our modern number system—except that instead of using different marks for larger numbers, we simply use a different symbol for each number up to nine, and then put the symbols in different positions for the larger numbers.

The early civilizations also developed mathematical skills. First, there was arithmetic. This is the art of working things out by numbers —by addition, subtraction, multiplication, and division. Arithmetic is the oldest of all the mathematical skills. We know that the Babylonians and Sumerians were skilled in arithmetic at

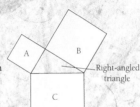

◀ SUMERIAN ACCOUNTANTS
The accountants of the ancient civilization of Sumeria may have written down the first numbers over 6,000 years ago. To keep track of tax accounts and payments, they scratched marks on soft clay tablets. The tablets hardened to make a permanent record.

THE GREAT GEOMETERS
The first great masters of geometry were the ancient Greeks, such as Pythagoras, Eudoxus, and, in particular, Euclid, who lived between about 330 and 275B.C. Geometry is actually a Greek word meaning "earth measurement." Euclid's book *Elements* was such a brilliantly thorough study of geometry that it became the framework for geometry for thousands of years. Even today, mathematicians still refer to all the geometry of flat surfaces—lines, points, shapes, and solids—as Euclidean geometry.

▶ EARLY GEOMETRY
Most basic geometry is about lines and the angles between them—and how they make up two kinds of shape, or figure: circles and polygons. The Greek geometers used to analyze these shapes in particular ways. They might try to calculate the area of a triangle, for instance, or work out the relationship between particular angles.

◀ PYTHAGORAS
Pythagoras of Samos (560–480B.C.) was one of the first great mathematicians. He is a rather mysterious figure, who believed that numbers were the perfect basis of life. He is most famous for his theory about right-angled triangles. His theory showed that if you square the two sides next to the right angle, the two add up to the third side squared. (Squaring simply means multiplying a number by itself.) This was expressed by Pythagoras in the following, famous formula;

A×A + B×B = C×C
or
$A^2 + B^2 = C^2$

A

B

Right-angled triangle

C

least 5,000 years ago. Babylonian schoolchildren learned how to multiply and divide, and they used arithmetical tables to help with complex sums.

Arithmetic was developed to keep the accounts that were the key to power in the ancient civilizations. Accounts and arithmetic were vital. For example, they helped to work out how much tax people owed. Many of those skilled in arithmetic were highly honored. In fact, they were often feared, for when mathematicians first learned to make quick mathematic calculations it seemed like magic. The arithmetic processes developed in ancient China seemed so tricky and clever that they were still being used by Chinese "mind-readers" in the variety shows of Europe in the early 20th century.

Another skill was geometry, which is the mathematics of shapes. It was probably first invented to help people work out the area of their land. Geometry was developed by the ancient Egyptians over 4,000 years ago to help them build perfect pyramids.

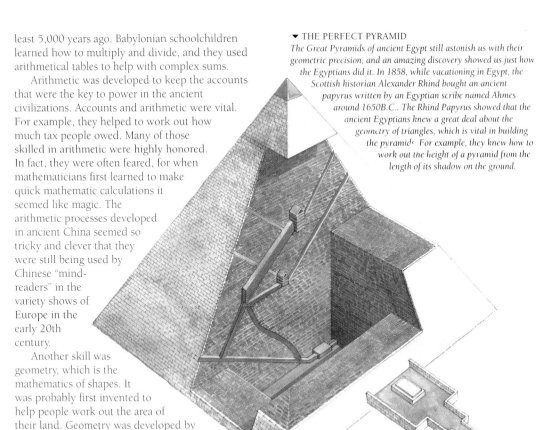

▼ THE PERFECT PYRAMID
The Great Pyramids of ancient Egypt still astonish us with their geometric precision, and an amazing discovery showed us just how the Egyptians did it. In 1858, while vacationing in Egypt, the Scottish historian Alexander Rhind bought an ancient papyrus written by an Egyptian scribe named Ahmes around 1650B.C.. The Rhind Papyrus showed that the ancient Egyptians knew a great deal about the geometry of triangles, which is vital in building the pyramids. For example, they knew how to work out the height of a pyramid from the length of its shadow on the ground.

◀ TRIANGULAR FRIEZE
The ancient Greeks were fascinated by perfect geometric shapes, which is reflected in their elegant temples. These graceful buildings were among the first to be built using geometric rules, with beautifully proportioned rectangles crowned by triangular friezes. At this time, geometry not only was used in the building of temples, it was the basis for practical engineering too. In fact, much of our knowledge of geometry is based on the theories of ancient Greeks.

Key Dates

- 1500B.C. Babylonians develop a number system.
- 530B.C. Pythagoras devises his theory about right-angled triangles.
- 300B.C. Euclid writes his *Elements of Geometry*, the most influential mathematics book ever written.
- 300B.C. The Hindus develop their own number system.
- 220B.C. Archimedes finds a way of measuring the volume of spheres.
- 200B.C. Appolonius analyzes slices across cones—parabolas and ellipses.
- A.D.662 Hindu number system develops into decimal system we now use.

Star Gazing

▲ PTOLEMY
Ptolemy was the great Alexandrian astronomer whose books were the definitive guide to astronomy for 1,500 years.

ASTRONOMY DATES BACK TO the earliest days of humankind, when prehistoric hunters gazed up at the sky to work out which night might give them a full moon for hunting. When people began to settle down to farm, 10,000 years ago, astronomy helped farmers to know when seasons would come and go. Indeed, astronomy played such a vital role in early civilizations that astronomers were often high priests. Many ancient monuments have strong links with astronomy. The standing stones in Stonehenge in England, for instance, are aligned with the rising sun on the solstices, the longest and shortest days of the year. Shafts in Egypt's Great Pyramids point at the star group called Orion.

By the time the ancient Greek astronomer Hipparchus of Rhodes (170–127B.C.) began to study the sky, astronomy was already an ancient art. Hipparchus was a skilled observer, but much of his work was based on old Babylonian records rescued from the ruins of the Persian Empire by Alexander the Great. Even so, his achievement was stupendous. He was the first great astronomer, and he laid the foundations for astronomy for almost 2,000 years.

Excited by spotting a new star in 134B.C., Hipparchus began to make a catalog of the 850 stars whose positions were then known. This catalog, adapted by Ptolemy, was still being used in the 16th century. Hipparchus also compared stars by giving each one a "Magnitude" from one to six, depending on how bright it looked. The

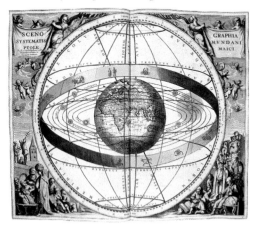

▲ PTOLEMY'S MAP
Early European maps were based on a work called Geography, *by the astronomer Ptolemy. It was because Ptolemy underestimated the size of the world that Columbus set out for Asia, sailing west across the Atlantic. This, then, inspired his discovery of the Americas.*

THE CONSTELLATIONS
To help find their way around the night sky, astronomers in ancient Babylon and Egypt looked for patterns of stars, or constellations. They named each star pattern after a mythical figure. On star maps, you often see these figures drawn over the stars, as if the stars were a giant "painting by numbers" book.

There is no real link between the stars in a constellation; they simply look close together. But the system is so effective that astronomers still use it, though they have added a few extra constellations. Each ancient civilization had its own names for constellations, and the names we use today come from Greek myths. The names are written, not in Greek, but in their Roman (Latin) equivalent, such as Cygnus (the Swan) and Ursa Major (the Great Bear).

▲ NORTHERN HEMISPHERE
These are some of the 88 constellations, or star groups, that are recognized by astronomers today. There are many other stars in the sky; the constellations simply make groups of the brightest stars.

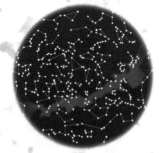

▲ SOUTHERN HEMISPHERE
A different set of constellations is visible from the Southern Hemisphere (half of the world). Indeed, many, such as Crux (the Southern Cross), would have been completely unknown to ancient Greeks.

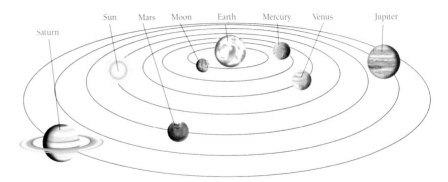

Many of the earliest astronomical records were kept by the Babylonians, who kept records on clay tablets like this one.

brightest star is Sirius (the Dog Star), which he called a First-Magnitude star; the faintest star was called a Sixth-Magnitude star. The idea of star magnitude is very important to astronomers even today, although the scale has been refined.

Hipparchus measured things in the sky very exactly, considering that he had only his own eyes to guide him. He made some amazingly precise measurements of the movements of the heavens. He calculated the length of a year, for instance, to within less than seven minutes. He also discovered that the relative positions of the stars on the equinoxes (March 21 and September 23) slowly shift around, and worked out that they take 26,000 years to return to the same place.

Sadly, hardly any of Hipparchus' work survives as he

▲ THE WANDERERS
Early astronomers such as Ptolemy knew that the world was round, but they believed that the Earth was the center of the Universe and everything revolved around it. They knew of only five planets— Mercury, Venus, Mars, Jupiter, and Saturn.

The early astronomers had no telescopes, so the planets looked just like stars, only they were brighter. What makes planets different is that the position of the stars in the night sky is fixed and they move only as the Earth turns. The planets, however, wander through the sky like the Sun and the Moon. This is why they are called planets, which is the Greek word for "wanderers."

wrote it. We know of it because it was developed by the astronomer Ptolemy (A.D.90–170), who wrote four books summarizing Greek astronomical ideas in the 2nd century A.D., including *Almagest* (Arabic for "The Greatest"). These books became the cornerstone of Western and Arab astronomy until the 16th century.

◄ EGYPTIAN ASTRONOMY
Here you can see an Egyptian drawing of the goddess Nut holding up the sky. The ancient Egyptians relied on astronomy to give them times and dates. They performed some religious ceremonies, for instance, at certain times during the night when the constellations reached a particular place in the sky.

The most important date was the time when Sirius, the brightest star in the sky, appeared after being hidden behind the Sun for many months. This date was important as it coincided with the annual floods of the river Nile, which made the Egyptian soils fertile.

Key Dates

- 2800B.C. The ancient Egyptian astronomer Imhotep aligns the first great pyramid perfectly with the Sun.

- 2500B.C. The ancient Egyptians devise a 365-day calendar.

- 550B.C. Greek astronomer Anaximander suggests that the Earth is a globe hanging in space.

- c.200B.C. Eratosthenes calculates the size of the Earth.

- 134B.C. Hipparchus catalogs 850 stars and devises a magnitude scale for stars.

- A.D.140 In *Almagest* Ptolemy describes the motions of the planets and catalogs stars and planets.

The First Scientist

▲ ARCHIMEDES
The great scientist Archimedes was killed when the Romans invaded Syracuse. Some say he was then working on a theory.

Archimedes was the world's first great scientist. Of course, others had studied scientific subjects before, but Archimedes was the first to think about problems in the scientific way that we now take for granted. He came up with abstract theories that could be proved or disproved by practical experiments and by mathematical calculations.

Archimedes lived in Syracuse in Sicily, which was a Greek colony at the time. He was born there around 285B.C., and spent most of his life in the city studying geometry and inventing all kinds of fantastic machines. These included the famous Archimedes' screw (a device for pumping water) and many war machines which he built for the defense of Syracuse. Archimedes was regarded with awe in his lifetime, and there are many stories about him.

The most famous is about a task that the king of Syracuse once set him. The king wanted to know if his crown was pure gold—or if the crafty goldsmith had mixed in some cheaper metal, as he suspected. Archimedes was thinking about

this tricky problem in his bath one day when suddenly he noticed how the water level rose the deeper he sank into the bath. The story goes that he leaped out of his bath and ran naked through the streets to the king, shouting at the top of his voice "Eureka! Eureka!," which means "I've got it! I've got it!" Later, he showed the king his idea. First, he immersed in water a piece of gold that weighed the same as the crown. Then he immersed the crown itself and discovered that the water level was different. Archimedes then concluded that the

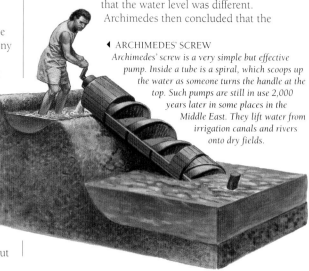

◀ ARCHIMEDES' SCREW
Archimedes' screw is a very simple but effective pump. Inside a tube is a spiral, which scoops up the water as someone turns the handle at the top. Such pumps are still in use 2,000 years later in some places in the Middle East. They lift water from irrigation canals and rivers onto dry fields.

FLOATING AND SINKING

One of Archimedes' great breakthroughs was the discovery that an object weighs less in water than in air—which is why you can lift a quite heavy person when in a swimming pool. The reason for this "buoyancy" is the natural upward push, or upthrust, of the water.

When an object is immersed in water, its weight pushes down. But the water, as Archimedes realized, pushes back up with a force equal to the weight of water the object pushes out of the way. So the object sinks until its weight is exactly equal to the upthrust of the water, at which point it floats. So objects that weigh less than the water displaced will float, and those that weigh more will sink.

▲ BUOYANCY
If you drop a barrel weighing 100g into water, it will sink until it displaces (pushes out of the way) a volume of water weighing 100g. It floats at this point because the upthrust created by pushing 100g of water out of the way exactly balances with the weight of the barrel.

▲ WHY SHIPS FLOAT
When the first iron ships were made in the 19th century, many people were convinced they would sink, because iron is too heavy to float. They were right; iron is too heavy to float. But iron and steel ships float because their hulls are full of air, and so they can safely sink until enough water is displaced to match the weight of the iron in the hull.

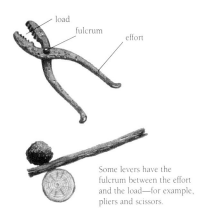

load
fulcrum
effort

Some levers have the fulcrum between the effort and the load—for example, pliers and scissors.

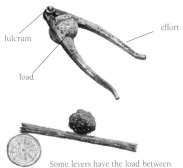

fulcrum
effort
load

Some levers have the load between the effort and the fulcrum—for example nutcrackers, wheelbarrows, and screwdrivers.

load
effort
fulcrum

Some levers have the effort between the load and the fulcrum—for example, sugar tongs.

crown was not pure gold, because the difference in water levels showed that the crown had a different volume from the gold, although they were the same weight. This proved that it must have included a different metal. The goldsmith was executed.

Whether this story is true or not, it is typical of Archimedes' amazingly neat and elegant scientific solutions to awkward questions. He also tried to approach problems mathematically. He was probably not the first to realize that if you put a weight on each end of a seesaw, the lighter weight must be farther away if the two weights are to balance. Archimedes, though, showed that the ratio of the weights goes down in exact mathematical proportion to the distance they must be from the pivot of the seesaw—and he proved this also mathematically. In the same way, he had the brilliant insight that every object has a center of gravity—a

▲ LEVERS AND FORCES
Archimedes' brilliant insight was to analyze mathematically an everyday tool such as a lever. If a lever, such as a plank of wood, pivots around one point, called the fulcrum, the effort you apply on one side of the fulcrum can move a load on the other side. What Archimedes found was that the load you could move with a certain amount of effort depended exactly on the relative distance of the effort and load from the fulcrum. Working out load, force, distance and so on mathematically is now one of the cornerstones of science.

single point from which all its weight seems to hang—and he proved it mathematically.

Sadly, much of Archimedes' work has been lost. Yet his approach to science—using mathematics to understand the physical world—is the basis of the most advanced science today. Almost 1,900 years after Archimedes' death, the great Italian scientist Galileo said, "Without Archimedes I could have achieved nothing."

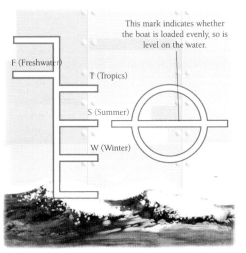

F (Freshwater)
T (Tropics)
S (Summer)
W (Winter)

This mark indicates whether the boat is loaded evenly, so is level on the water.

◀ PLIMSOLL MARK
The density of water (how tightly together its particles are packed) changes depending on its temperature and on whether it is fresh (non-salty) or sea water. Ships float higher in cold or salty water because it is more dense and creates more upthrust.

Some ships are marked with a set of lines, called a Plimsoll mark, to show the safe levels to which cargo can be loaded on board —in the tropics, in freshwater, in summer, and in winter.

Key Dates

- c.450B.C. Empedocles suggests that all substances are made from four elements: earth, air, fire, and water.

- c.335B.C. Theophrastus writes the first scientific book on plants.

- c.350B.C. Aristotle lays down rules for science.

- 250B.C. Archimedes discovers principles of buoyancy and forms mathematical rules for levers.

- c.A.D.70 Hero of Alexander invents a pump, a fountain, and a steam turbine.

- c.A.D.100 Chinese thinker Zhang Heng makes a seismoscope to record earthquakes.

Roman Engineers

▲ ROMAN BUILDINGS
This temple is an excellent example of Roman architecture. To create buildings such as this, the Roman's would use bricks to form a strong and long-lasting structure.

ANCIENT ROME HAD few of the great thinkers that made ancient Greece so remarkable. However, it had many clever, practical men, and the Romans were the greatest engineers and builders of the ancient world. Their bridges, roads, and aqueducts are marvels of ingenious, efficient large-scale construction, and many of them are still standing today, over 2,000 years later. Some, such as the eight aqueducts that supply Rome with water, are still in use, working as well as they ever did. It is hard to imagine many modern structures lasting so long.

Much of the Romans' engineering was connected with their military conquests, and engineers traveled with the armies to build roads and bridges. A sound knowledge of engineering was an essential skill for an officer, and soldiers provided much of the labor for the major construction works. Whenever the Romans conquered a new territory, one of the army's first tasks was to lay out cities to a standard plan, build roads to supply the army, and lay on a clean water supply.

The Romans inherited some of their construction techniques from the Greeks and the Etruscans. They added to the Greek knowledge and pushed Greek techniques to new levels, adding a number of features of their own. One of the keys to Roman engineering was the arch. The arch is a simple but clever way of making strong bridges. A flat piece of stone across two posts can take only so much weight before snapping. But in an arch the stones are pushed harder together when weight is placed on them, so the arch actually becomes stronger.

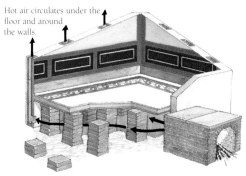

Hot air circulates under the floor and around the walls.

▲ UNDERFLOOR HEATING
We tend to think of central heating as a modern invention, but many Roman villas (houses) had a space under the floor called a hypocaust. Warm air from the hot bricks of a furnace circulated through this space, keeping the floor warm and the house very cozy.

ROMAN ROADS

None of the Romans' engineering achievements has had more impact than their road system. The Romans began building roads in 334B.C., and by the time their empire was at its peak they had laid down more than 53,000 miles of roads, including the famous Appian Way running 410 miles through Italy.

During this time most roads were simple, rough dirt tracks, which were impassable with mud in winter. By contrast, the Romans laid smooth, hard-surfaced roads which cut as straight as an arrow across marshes, lakes, gorges, and hills. Using these roads, their soldiers could move around the empire with astonishing speed.

▲ ROMAN ROUTES
Even today, roads in many parts of the world quickly become impassable in bad weather. The Romans, however, built their roads to be used in all seasons. They built strong stone bridges high above rivers, and raised roads, on embankments called aggers, above ground that was liable to flooding. They even made grooves in the road to guide trucks.

Another feature of Roman engineering was cement. The Romans made bricks on an unprecedented scale, and Roman bridges and buildings are the first great brick structures. At first, the structures were mortared together with a mixture of sand, lime, and water. In the 2nd century B.C. a new ingredient was added: volcanic sand found near the modern town of Pozzuoli in Italy. This ingredient, now called pozzolana, turned mortar into an incredibly tough cement which hardens even underwater. Pozzolanic mortars were so strong and cheap that the Romans began to build with cement only and dispense with the bricks. Eventually, they added stones to make concrete.

With the arch and pozzolanic cement, the Romans could build bridges and aqueducts on a massive scale, such as the famous Pont du Gard, near Nîmes in France, and the 2,560-foot-long Segovia aqueduct in Spain. The fact that these bridges have survived almost 2,000 years testifies to both their strength and their durability.

▶ BUILDING AN AQUEDUCT
Building a Roman aqueduct was a huge job involving hundreds and sometimes thousands of men. To build each arch, the engineers constructed a framework of wood, on which they laid the stones. Towering scaffolds of wood enabled them to build rows of arches which were 300 feet or more high.

▶ A ROMAN ROAD
To build their roads, the Romans laid a deep, solid foundation of large stone. They covered this with a smooth surface of flat stones, with a raised center, or "crown," so that water would drain off on either side. They also dug ditches along the sides of the road to carry the water away.

Key Dates

- c.3200B.C. The wheel is invented in Sumeria.
- 2800B.C. The ancient Egyptians build the first pyramid.
- 1470B.C. Pharaoh Sesostris builds first Suez Canal, linking the Nile River to the Red Sea.
- 480B.C. Xerxes of Persia builds a bridge of boats across the Hellespont.
- 312B.C. The Appian Way, the first great Roman road, is built.
- 221–206B.C. The Great Wall of China is built.
- c.A.D.200 By this time the Romans have built over 53,000 miles of roads.

Where and When

▲ SHIP'S COMPASS
The compasses that ships use utilize a suspended, magnetized needle that aligns itself in a north-south direction with the Earth's magnetic field.

I N THE MIDDLE AGES THE Europeans knew little of the world. Maps were inaccurate and showed Asia, to the east, only vaguely. To the south, Africa faded off into a mystery land filled with monsters and dangerous peoples. To the west there was nothing at all. It was still not absolutely certain that the world was round. Perhaps the world ended in empty space? Even charts of Europe itself were so inaccurate and navigation methods so unreliable that ships stayed in sight of land to be sure of finding their way.

Then, in the 14th century, the great Mongol Empire in Asia collapsed. The roads to China and the East, along which silks and spices were brought, were cut off. So bold European mariners set out westward to find their way to the East by sea. From 1400, ship after ship sailed from Europe. At first they ventured south around the unknown west of Africa in small ships called caravels. Many of these mariners were Portuguese, sent out by Prince Henry "the Navigator" (1394–1460) from his base at Sagres. They pushed on, cape by cape, until Bartolomeu Dias rounded Africa's southern tip in 1488. Nine years later, Vasco da Gama sailed right around to India. In the

▼ THE CARAVEL
Up until the 15th century, most European ships were square-rigged, which meant that they could sail only in much the same direction as the wind. Most of the great explorers, including Columbus, used a small revolutionary ship called a caravel, which had triangular "lateen" sails adopted from Arab dhows. With these sails, a caravel could sail almost directly into the wind.

THE SEARCH FOR LONGITUDE

Finding longitude was a problem in navigation for a long time. In theory you can work it out from the Sun's position in the sky, comparing this to its position at the same time at a longitude you know. However, you must know the exact time. Huygens had made an accurate pendulum clock in the 1670s, but it was too sensitive to keep good time aboard a tossing ship. The solution was the chronometer, a very accurate, stormproof clock made in the 1720s by John Harrison (1693–1776). It used balance springs, rather than a pendulum, to keep time.

◀ HUYGENS'S CLOCK
The pendulum clock, invented by Christiaan Huygens in the 1670s, was the world's first accurate timepiece.

◀ HARRISON'S CHRONOMETER
It took John Harrison decades to persuade the authorities that his chronometer was indeed the solution to the longitude problem. This is his second version.

▲ LATITUDE
Latitude says how far north or south you are in degrees. Lines of latitude are called parallels because they form rings around the Earth parallel to the Equator. You can work out latitude from the Sun's height in the sky at noon. The higher it is, the nearer the Equator you are.

▲ LONGITUDE
Longitude says how far east or west you are in degrees. Lines of longitude, or meridians, run from pole to pole, dividing the world like orange segments. You can work out your longitude from the time it is when the Sun is at its highest.

meantime, in 1492, Christopher Columbus took a great gamble and set out west across the open Atlantic, hoping to reach China. Instead, he found the New World of the Americas waiting to be explored. Finally, in 1522, fewer than 90 years after the voyages of discovery had begun, Ferdinand Magellan's ship *Victoria* sailed all the way around the world. Now there could be no doubt: the world is round.

Maps improved vastly as each voyage brought new knowledge, and map "projections" were devised to show the round world on flat paper and parchment. Yet these early projections helped sailors little, since a straight course at sea was an elaborate line on the map. In 1552 the Dutch mapmaker Gerhardus Mercator invented a new projection. It treated the map of the world as if it were projected onto a cylinder, which could then be rolled out and laid flat. Although Mercator's projection made countries near the poles look far too big, it enabled sailors to plot a straight course by compass simply by drawing a straight line on the map.

At the same time, navigation at sea made startling progress. Early sailors had steered entirely by the stars—they had only a vague idea where they were during the day, and no idea at all if the sky clouded over. From the 12th century on, European sailors used a magnetic needle to find north at all times. This however, gave them only a direction to steer; it did not tell them where they were. From the 14th century, sailors used an astrolabe to get an idea of their latitude—how far north or south of the Equator—by measuring the height of a star or the Sun at noon. The great breakthrough came with the invention of the cross-staff in the 16th century. Sailors used it to measure the angle between the horizon and the Pole Star and so work out their latitude precisely. Now the problem was longitude—how far east or west they were. For centuries, the only way to work out a ship's longitude was to guess how far it had come by "dead reckoning." This involved trailing a knotted rope in the water to keep a constant track of the ship's speed. However, this was not very accurate, so the problem of longitude was to tax some of the greatest minds over the next few centuries.

▶ GREENWICH *The great observatory at Greenwich, London, was set up in 1675. Its brief from King Charles II was to map the movements of the heavens so accurately that the longitude problem could be solved. The problem was not solved here, but the observatory sits on the Prime Meridian, the first line of longitude.*

▲ HOW FAR NORTH?
The mirror sextant was developed in the mid-1700s from the cross-staff to measure latitude accurately. It became the main navigation aid for sailors until the days of electronic technology after World War II. It has one mirror which you point at the horizon and another mirror which you adjust until the Sun (or a star) is reflected in it at exactly the same height as the horizon. The degree of adjustment you need to make to the second mirror gives the latitude. The sextant gets its name from its shape, which is one-sixth of a circle.

Key Dates

- 1488 Bartolomeu Dias sails around the southern tip of Africa.
- 1492 Christopher Columbus sails across the Atlantic.
- 1497 Vasco da Gama sails around Africa to India.
- 1497 John Cabot discovers Canada while trying to find a way to Asia.
- 1501 Amerigo Vespucci realizes that South America is a whole new continent.
- 1513 Vasco de Balboa of Spain sails on the Pacific Ocean.
- 1519 Ferdinand Magellan leads the first voyage around the world.

The Great Anatomists

NOTHING IS CLOSER TO us than the human body, yet it has taken as long to explore it as it has to explore the Earth. For thousands of years medicine was based as much on superstition as on research. The first doctor that we know about was Imhotep, who lived in ancient Egypt 4,600 years ago. People traveled from far and wide to be treated by him, and after his death he was declared to be a god. The greatest physician of the ancient world was the Roman Galen, born around

▼ DA VINCI'S ANATOMICAL DRAWINGS
To draw human figures exactly, many artists in the Renaissance began to study human anatomy for themselves. Some, such as Da Vinci, made their own dissections, and their knowledge of the human body often outstripped that of physicians.

▲ LEONARDO DA VINCI
Da Vinci (1452–1519) is best known for his few master paintings, such as the Mona Lisa *and the* Last Supper. *His curiosity led him to study everything from human anatomy to astronomy with the same remarkable insight.*

THE POWER OF THE MICROSCOPE

Until the microscope was invented, in around 1590, people never suspected that many things were far too small for the eye to see. Soon, using a simple microscope made with a drop of water, the Dutch scientist Anton van Leeuwenhoek found that the world is full of tiny microorganisms such as bacteria.

In the 1660s the Italian physician Marcello Malphigi (1628–1694) began to use a microscope to study the human body. He made many discoveries of tiny structures such as the tastebuds on the tongue. He did not, however, restrict himself to the study of humans, but he studied plants and animals in great detail as well.

▼ MICROSCOPES
Early microscopes magnified things many times by combining two lenses. One lens, called the objective lens, bends light rays apart to create an enlarged image; but this image is still very small. A second lens, called the eyepiece lens, acts like a magnifying glass to make this tiny image visible.

A.D.130. Like his contemporaries, Galen learned about the body by studying ancient manuscripts, but he also took a scientific approach and cut up animals to see how their bodies worked. He recorded his findings in many books describing the skeleton, the muscles, and the nerves. Respect for Galen was so great that for more than 1,000 years, doctors would consult Galen's books rather than look at a body.

During the Renaissance in Italy in the 15th and 16th centuries, physicians began to consider that it might be better to look at real bodies, rather than at Galen's texts. They retrieved dead bodies from graveyards and cut them up to see exactly how they were put together. This is called dissection. The focus of this revolution was the University of Padua, where a brilliant German, Andreas Vesalius (1514–1564), was professor of surgery and anatomy. (Anatomy is the study of the way the human body is put together.) When dissection had been done in the past, it was usually done for the physicians by a butcher. Vesalius, though, began dissecting corpses himself, and he asked the Flemish artist Jan van Calcar to draw very accurately what he found. In 1543, Vesalius published his findings in a textbook of anatomy called *De Humani Corporis Fabrica* ("On the Structure of the Human Body"), which became the most influential medical book ever written.

Inspired by Vesalius's work, other physicians began to make their own dissections. Piece by piece, a very detailed picture of human anatomy began to build up. In the 1550s, for instance, Vesalius's colleague Gabriel Fallopio (1523–1562) discovered the tubes that link a

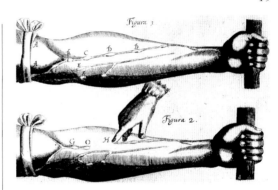

▲ BLOOD CIRCULATION
The English physician William Harvey (1578–1657) was one of the many great scientists who studied at the University of Padua in the 1500s and 1600s. Harvey's great insight was to realize that blood flows out from the heart through arteries and back through veins, making a complete circulation of the blood.

female's ovaries to the uterus. These are now known as the Fallopian tubes. He also identified various other parts of the female reproductive system. Another colleague, Matteo Corti, discovered minute structures in the inner ear.

Gradually, physicians began also to learn about physiology (the science of the workings of the body). In 1590, for example, Santorio Sanctorius showed how to measure pulse and body temperature. In 1628 William Harvey showed that the heart is a pump and that blood circulates round and round the body. In this way the foundations for our current knowledge of the human body were built bit by bit.

▶ MALPHIGI
Marcello Malphigi was the first person to apply the power of the newly invented microscope to the human body. He made the first microscopic studies of human tissues, discovering the tiny structures present in the body. In 1661 Malphigi discovered capillaries, the minute blood vessels that were the missing link in Harvey's blood circulation.

Marcellus Malpighius

Key Dates

- c.480 B.C. Hippocrates, one of the first great doctors, practices in Greece.

- c. A.D. 130 Galen writes his medical treatises.

- 1543 Vesalius publishes his book *De Humani Corporis Fabrica*.

- 1550 Gabriel Fallopius studies the human body in minute detail.

- 1590 Santorio Sanctorius creates science of physiology and shows how to measure pulse and temperature.

- 1628 William Harvey shows how the heart circulates blood.

- 1661 Marcello Malphigi sees tiny blood vessels called capillaries under a microscope.

The Moving Earth

▲ COPERNICUS
The astronomer Copernicus spent most of his life studying old astronomical texts at Frauenberg Cathedral in Germany. His radical theories shook the world.

U NTIL THE 16TH century, nearly everyone was certain that the Earth was at the center of the Universe and that the Moon, the Sun, the planets, and the stars revolved around it. Then a Polish astronomer, Nicolaus Copernicus, began to think there was something strange about the path of the planets through the sky.

Most of the time, the planets follow a smooth, curved path, but every now and then some of them perform a small backward loop through the sky. Ancient astronomers, including the brilliant Ptolemy, had explained this by suggesting that everything in the Universe worked by an ingenious system of epicycles, or wheels within wheels. This elaborate system did not quite ring true with Copernicus. He noted, for example, that the stars seem sometimes nearer and sometimes farther away. "Why should this be?" he asked.

Then Copernicus had a simple but brilliant idea. What if the Earth was not the fixed center of the Universe but was one of the planets revolving around

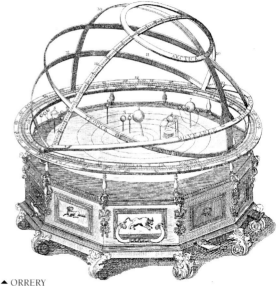

▲ ORRERY
Once people accepted the idea that the Earth was just one of the planets circling the Sun, they became fascinated by how this system worked. In 1710 a Scottish clockmaker named George Graham built a clockwork model to show how the planets moved. He built the model for his patron, the 4th Earl of Orrery. Orreries, as they came to be known, were soon very popular.

the Sun? Then the strange movement of the planets and the varying distance of the stars would be explained very simply. He wrote his ideas in a book called *De Revolutionibus Orbium Coelestium* ("On the Revolutions of the Heavenly Spheres"), which was published just after he died in 1543.

GALILEO'S TELESCOPE

Galileo did not invent the telescope, but he was the first person to make one for looking at the night sky. He encountered an extraordinary amount of prejudice and skepticism. One professor said that he refused to waste his time looking through this silly device "to see what no one but Galileo has seen. Besides, it gives me a headache." "It's all a trick!" said others.

When an excited Galileo tried to show the professors at Bologna the four moons of Jupiter which he had seen through his telescope, all the "most excellent men and noble doctors" insisted that "the instrument lies!" Father Clavius, the professor of mathematics, laughed and said he would show them the moons of Jupiter, too, if he had time to paint them onto the lens.

▲ GALILEO
Galileo Galilei (1564–1642) was one of the greatest scientists of all time. He made many important scientific discoveries, but none that caused as much controversy as his support for Copernicus's ideas.

▶ POWERFUL TELESCOPES
In 1609 Galileo heard of the invention of the telescope in the Netherlands. He quickly learned how to make his own telescope. His telescopes were increasingly powerful, magnifying up to 20 times.

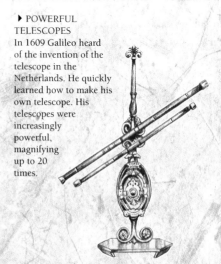

No single idea in history has changed our view of the Universe, and our place in it, quite so much. At first, only a few astronomers paid much attention to Copernicus's new theory. After all, people had been publishing crazy ideas for centuries. Then early in the 17th century, the famous Italian scientist Galileo began to look at the night sky with a new device called a telescope. What Galileo saw through his telescope proved that Copernicus's ideas were not just an interesting theory—they were really true.

Galileo saw two things that confirmed this view for him. The first was the fact that he could see four moons circling Jupiter—the first proof that the Earth is not at the center of things. The second was the fact that he could see that Venus has phases like our Moon. (Phases are the way the Moon seems to change shape as we see its bright sunlit side from a different angle.) The nature of Venus's phases showed that it must be moving around the Sun, not the Earth.

Catholic teaching at that time was based on the idea that the Earth was the fixed center of the Universe. When Galileo published his findings in a book called *The Starry Messenger* in 1513, he was declared a heretic by the cardinals in Rome. When threatened

with torture, Galileo was forced to deny that the Earth moves. Legend says that he muttered *"Eppur si muove"* ("Yet it does move") later. The Catholic Church did not retract its sentence on Galileo until October 13, 1992.

▼ COPERNICUS'S MAP OF THE HEAVENS
Copernicus's map showed that the Earth was not at the center of the Universe and gave us the "heliocentric," or Sun-centered, Universe. Now we know, of course, that not even the Sun is the center of the Universe. It is just one of many billions of stars.

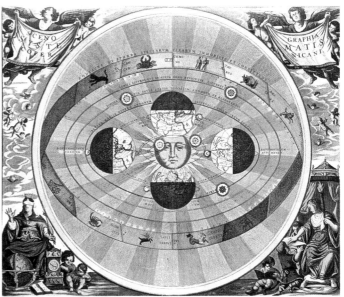

◀ JUPITER'S MOONS
In January 1610, Galileo was looking at the planet Jupiter through his telescope when he saw what could only be four tiny moons circling it. Up until then, most people thought everything in the Universe circled the Earth. Yet here were four moons circling just one of the planets in the solar system. Jupiter is now known to have 16 moons. The four that Galileo saw are called Galilean moons.

Key Dates

- 300 B.C. Greek astronomer Aristarchus suggests that the Earth revolves around the Sun.

- 1543 Copernicus suggests that the Earth circles the Sun.

- 1550 Johann Kepler recognizes that the planets follow elliptical, not circular, paths.

- 1610 With his telescope Galileo sees mountains on the Moon and four moons orbiting the planet Jupiter.

- 1665 Isaac Newton uses the theory of gravity to explain how the planets move.

- 1781 William Herschel discovers the planet Uranus.

Force and Motion

▲ ISAAC NEWTON
Isaac Newton (1642–1727) showed the link between force and motion in his three laws of motion. He realized that a force he called gravity makes things fall and keeps the planets orbiting the Sun.

THE 17TH CENTURY WAS THE first real age of science, when brilliant men such as Galileo, Huygens, Boyle, Newton, Liebnitz, and Leeuwenhoek made many important discoveries. Of all their achievements, however, perhaps none was as important as the understanding of forces and motion.

The philosophers of ancient Greece had known a great deal about "statics"—things that are not moving. When it came to movement, or "dynamics," however, they were often baffled. They could see, for instance, that a plow moves because the ox pulls it and that an arrow flies because of the force of the bow. But how, they wondered, did an arrow keep on flying through the air after it left the bow—if there was nothing to pull it along? The Greek philosopher Aristotle made his commonsense assertion that you must have a force to keep something moving—just as your bike will slow to a halt if you stop pedaling.

Yet common sense can be wrong, and it took the genius of Galileo and Newton to realiz

▼ THE TOWER OF PISA
Galileo was the first to appreciate that gravity accelerates any falling object downward by exactly the same amount. In other words, things will fall at the same speed no matter how heavy they are. Legend has it that he demonstrated this by dropping two objects of different weights from the Leaning Tower of Pisa in Italy. The two objects would have hit the ground at the same time.

NEWTON AND GRAVITY

No one knew why planets circle around the Sun or why things fall to the ground until one day around 1665, when Newton was thinking in an orchard. As an apple fell to the ground, Newton wondered if the apple were not just falling but actually being pulled to the Earth by an invisible force. From this simple but brilliant idea, Newton developed his theory of gravity, a universal force that tries to pull all matter to together. Without gravity, the whole Universe would disintegrate.

Newton showed that the force of gravity is the same everywhere, and that the pull between two things depends on their mass (the amount of matter in them) and the square of the distance between them.

PHILOSOPHIÆ NATURALIS PRINCIPIA MATHEMATICA

Autore JS. NEWTON, Trin. Coll. Cantab. Soc. Matheseos Professore Lucasiano, & Societatis Regalis Sodali.

INPRIMATUR
S. PEPYS, Reg. Soc. PRÆSES.
Jul. 5. 1686.

LONDINI

Jussu Societatis Regiæ ac Typis Josephi Streater. Prostat apud plures Bibliopolas. Anno MDCLXXXVII.

▲ NEWTON'S PRINCIPIA
Newton's *Philosophiae naturalis principia mathematica* (The Mathematical Principles of Natural Philosophy), in which he set out the laws of motion, is the most influential science book ever written.

▶ BAROMETER
By the mid-1600s scientists knew about force and motion and about gravity. The picture of what made things move was completed when they learned about pressure. In 1644 one of Galileo's students, Evangelista Torricelli, showed that air is not empty space but a substance.

In a famous experiment, Torricelli showed that air has so much substance it can press hard enough to hold up a column of liquid mercury in a tube. In this experiment, Torricelli made the first barometer, the first device for measuring air pressure. Before long, he realized the value of the barometer for forecasting weather.

of experiments—notably rolling balls down slopes—Galileo realized that you do not need force to keep something moving. Exactly the opposite is true. Something will keep moving at the same speed unless a force slows it down. This is why an arrow flies on through the air. It falls to the ground only because the resistance of the air (a force) slows it down enough for gravity (another force) to pull it down. This is the idea of inertia. Galileo realized that there is no real difference between something that is moving at a steady speed and something that is not moving at all—both are unaffected by forces. But to make the object go faster or slower, or begin to move, a force is needed.

Further experiments, this time with swinging weights, led Galileo to a second crucial insight. If something moves faster, then the rate it accelerates depends on the strength of the force moving it faster

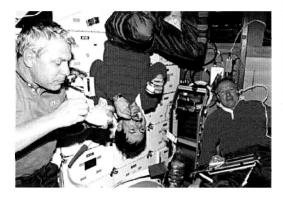

and how heavy the object is. A large force accelerates a light object rapidly, while a small force accelerates a heavy object slowly.

Galileo's ideas made huge leaps in the understanding of force and motion. In 1642, the year he died, another scientific genius, Isaac Newton, was born. It was Newton who drew these ideas together and laid the basis of the science of dynamics. In his remarkable book *Philosophiae naturalis principia mathematica* ("The Mathematical Principles of Natural Philosophy"), published in 1684, Newton established three fundamental laws, which together account for all types of motion.

The first two laws were Galileo's two insights about inertia and acceleration. Newton's third law showed that whenever a force pushes or pulls on one thing, it must push or pull on another thing equally in the opposite direction (see below). Newton's three laws gave scientists a clear understanding of how force and motion are related and a way of analyzing them mathematically. Morever, together with Newton's insight into the force of gravity (the pull between two things), these laws seemed to account for every single movement in the Universe, large or small—from the jumping of a flea to the movements of the planets.

◄ WEIGHTLESSNESS
In a spaceship orbiting the Earth, the crew floats weightless. You might think that gravity is not working, just as Newton had predicted. The reality is that gravity is in fact still acting as a force, but the spaceship is hurtling around the Earth so fast that its effects are cancelled out.

▼ THE THREE LAWS
Newton's laws of motion are involved in every single movement in the Universe. They can be seen in action in a frog jumping from a lily pad.

Newton's first law says that an object accelerates (or decelerates) only when a force is applied. In other words, you need force to make a still object move (inertia) or to make a moving object slow down or speed up (momentum). To jump from the lily pad, the frog needs to use the force of its leg muscles.

The second law says that the acceleration depends on the size of the force and the object's mass. So the frog will take off faster if it gives a stronger kick (or is less heavy).

The third law says that when a force pushes or acts one way, an equal force pushes in the opposite direction. So as the frog takes off, its kick pushes the lily pad back.

Key Dates

- 1638 Galileo publishes his theories on speed and forces.
- 1644 Evangelista Torricelli demonstrates the reality of air pressure and invents the barometer.
- 1646 Blaise Pascal shows how air pressure drops the higher you go.
- 1650 Otto von Guericke invents the air pump.
- 1660 Robert Boyle shows how the volume and pressure of a gas vary.
- 1686 Newton publishes his work *The Mathematical Principles of Natural Philosophy*. It contains his theory of gravity and three laws of motion.

Atoms and Matter

THANKS TO NEWTON AND Galileo, scientists in the 17th century knew a lot about how and why things moved; but they knew little about what things are made of. In ancient Greece 2,000 years earlier, philosophers thought all substances were made of just four basic things, or elements—earth, water, air, and fire. In the Middle Ages men called alchemists had tried heating and mixing substances to see how to change one into another. They discovered new substances such as nitric acid and sulfuric acid, but they still agreed with the idea of four elements.

The first chemist to really doubt this idea was the Irishman Robert Boyle (1627–1691), who carried out experiments with all kinds of substances. In his book *The Sceptical Chemist*, Boyle suggested that everything is made from a handful of basic substances, or "elements," each made up from a tiny lump called an "elementary corpuscle." Boyle believed that all the substances in the world are compounds made from these corpuscles joined together in different ways.

▲ JOSEPH PRIESTLEY
Joseph Priestley (1733–1804) is the English scientist who discovered the gas in air that Lavoisier later called oxygen. This is the gas we need to breathe and fire needs to burn.

▼ LAVOISIER IN HIS LABORATORY
Lavoisier's carefully weighed experiments showed that air, one of the four basic elements of the ancient Greeks, is actually a mixture of different gases, mainly oxygen and nitrogen. He also showed that another of the basic elements, water, is a compound of hydrogen and oxygen.

DALTON AND ATOMIC THEORY

The idea that all matter is really made of tiny particles called atoms was first suggested by the Greek philosopher Democritus in the 5th century B.C. Later, in the 17th century, it was championed by Boyle, with his elementary corpuscles.

The English chemist John Dalton (1766–1844) put forward the first real atomic theory and gave the first proof of it. By comparing the relative weights of the elements in different samples of different compounds (chemical combinations of elements), Dalton was able to deduce how much an atom of each element actually weighs.

DALTON'S MODEL OF WATER MOLECULES

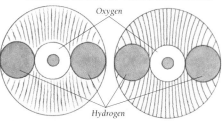

Oxygen

Hydrogen

▲ DALTON'S ATOMIC MODEL
Dalton's theory showed that compounds are formed when the atoms of one element join with the atoms of another. Dalton believed that water was made when a hydrogen atom links with an oxygen atom. Italian physicist Amedeo Avogadro later showed that each atom of oxygen joined with two hydrogen atoms, not one, to make water.

▼ DALTON'S ELEMENTS.
In 1808 Dalton published the first list of chemicals, complete with his estimated weights for individual atoms, or "atomic weights."

▶ MINER'S FRIEND
With the idea of chemical elements established, chemists raced to discover new ones. Dalton's 1803 notebooks show just 20 elements. By 1830 chemists knew of 55. Flamboyant English scientist Humphry Davy (1778–1829) discovered sodium and potassium and showed that chlorine and aluminum were elements. Davy is best remembered for inventing the miner's safety lamp, which greatly reduced the risk of explosions underground.

The alchemists believed that one substance could be changed into another—that was why they had searched for the "philosopher's stone," a substance that would transform ordinary "base" metal into gold. If Boyle's theory of elements were true, the alchemists were wrong; substances could only be mixed together differently but not actually changed. The scene was set for a controversy that raged throughout the 18th century.

The debate focused on burning. If you look at wood turning to ash as it burns, or at metal turning rusty, the alchemists argued, it seems quite clear that substances can change. An alchemist named Georg Stahl suggested in the early 18th century that anything burnable contains a special "active" substance called phlogiston, which dissolves into the air when it burns. If this is so, anything that burns must surely become lighter as it loses phlogiston. Does this happen?

A French chemist, Antoine Lavoisier (1743–1794), realized that the way to settle the argument was to weigh substances carefully before and after burning. In a brilliant experiment, Lavoisier burned a piece of tin inside a sealed container. The tin was actually heavier after burning—contrary to the phlogiston theory—but the air became lighter. So there was really no change in weight at all—substances were simply changing places! It was also clear that instead of losing something (phlogiston) to the air, the tin was taking something from it. Lavoisier later realized this was the gas oxygen, which had recently been discovered in England by scientist Joseph Priestley.

Lavoisier's experiment was a turning point in our understanding of matter, for three reasons. First, it put accurate scientific measurement firmly at the heart of chemistry. Second, it demolished the phlogiston theory and showed that burning is a process involving oxygen. Third, it showed that substances do not change even in a process as dramatic as burning; they simply change places. So Lavoisier put Boyle's idea of elements firmly on the map. Indeed, he made the first real list of chemical elements. Quite rightly, he has been called the father of modern chemistry.

◀ MENDELEYEV
Dmitri Mendeleyev was a Russian chemist who lived from 1834 to 1907. In the 1860s he realized that if the 60 elements known then were arranged in order of increasing atomic weight, then elements with similar chemical characteristics could be arranged in eight neat vertical groups. This arrangement, later known as the periodic table, has become central to our understanding of the elements. Scientists today continue to use Mendeleyev's table to assist them in their work and experiments.

Key Dates

- 1661 Robert Boyle introduces the idea of elements and compounds.

- 1756 Joseph Black deduces the presence of carbon dioxide in the air.

- 1774 Joseph Priestley discovers many new gases, including ammonia.

- 1784 Henry Cavendish shows that water is a compound of hydrogen and oxygen.

- 1789 Lavoisier writes the first list of elements and disproves the phlogiston theory.

- 1808 John Dalton proposes his atomic theory of chemical elements.

- 1818 Jöns Bezelius publishes the first table of atomic weights for the elements.

Factory and Furnace

▲ IRON BRIDGE
Iron was the new material of the Industrial Age. In 1779 the first all-iron bridge was built in Coalbrookdale in England.

UNTIL 1750, MOST people lived in country villages, raising animals and growing crops. Then two great revolutions started in Britain and changed things forever. A revolution in farming drove poor laborers off the land. A revolution in industry saw cottage crafts give way to great factories. People who were driven off the land came to work in the factories, and the first great industrial cities grew up.

These revolutions were fueled by the growth of European colonies and trade around the world. Colonies were vast new markets for goods such as clothes and eating utensils. In the past, people had made things slowly by hand. Now enterprising men realized they could make a fortune by producing huge quantities of goods quickly and cheaply for the new markets. They began to invent machines to speed things up, increase production, and reduce the number of people to be paid.

At first, the clothing industry was the main focus. Traditionally, yarn had been made by spinning together fibers, such as cotton, with a foot-driven spinning wheel. Cloth was woven from yarn on a loom, by hand. Then in

THE COMING OF WATERWAYS

The traditional horse and cart could not transport all the goods produced by the new factories, and within a few decades thousands of miles of canals were built across Europe. Using thousands of construction workers, these canals were then the biggest, most complex things ever built by humans.

▶ NEWCOMEN'S ENGINE
Newcomen's 1712 beam engine was the first practical steam engine. Steam drove a piston up and down to rock the beam which pumped water from the mines. It used a lot of coal but worked.

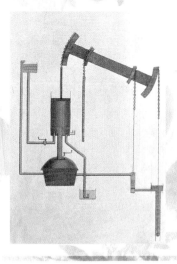

◀ SEVERN CANAL
The great canal-building era began in 1761 with James Brindley's Bridgewater Canal from Manchester, England. Soon the Grand Trunk Canal linked the rivers Mersey and Trent, and the Severn Canal linked the Thames and Bristol Channel. The area around Birmingham became the hub of a national canal network.

1733, John Kay built a machine called a flying shuttle. Kay's shuttle wove cloth so fast that the spinners could not make enough yarn. In 1764 Lancashire weaver James Hargreaves created the spinning jenny to spin yarn on eight spindles at once. This was a machine for home use, but a bigger breakthrough was Richard Arkwright's water frame of 1766. The water frame was a spinning machine driven by a water wheel. In 1771 Arkwright installed a series of water frames in a mill in Cromford in Derbyshire, England, to create the world's first large factory.

The early factories were water powered, but could they be powered by steam? Steam would be more powerful and there would be no need to locate factories by rivers. Thomas Savery had created a steam engine for pumping water out of mines in 1698, and a version developed by Newcomen in the 1720s was installed in many mines. Newcomen's engine was expensive to run, but in the 1780s James Watt created a cheaper engine. It gave power anywhere, and steam engines soon took over in factories.

The success of steam power depended on machine tools to shape metal, such as John Wilkinson's 1775 metal borer, and on iron and coal. Coal produced heat to make, or "smelt," iron. In the past iron had been smelted with charcoal. Then, in 1713, Abraham Darby found out how to smelt with coke, a kind of processed coal. Soon huge amounts of iron were churned out by coke-smelters. The combination of big steam-powered machines, cheap iron and coal proved unstoppable, and the quiet rural ways gave way to the big cities and noisy factories.

▼ THE INDUSTRIAL TOWN
The vast new towns of the Industrial Revolution, such as Birmingham and Leeds, were different from any town before. Noisy, smoky factories loomed over neatly packed rows of tiny brick houses—home to tens of thousands of factory workers. The coming of the railroads in the 1840s completed the picture.

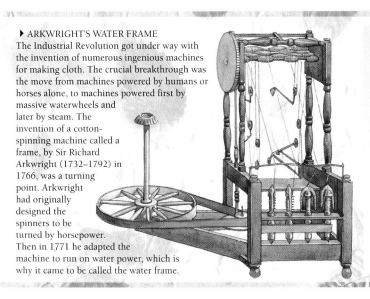

▶ ARKWRIGHT'S WATER FRAME
The Industrial Revolution got under way with the invention of numerous ingenious machines for making cloth. The crucial breakthrough was the move from machines powered by humans or horses alone, to machines powered first by massive waterwheels and later by steam. The invention of a cotton-spinning machine called a frame, by Sir Richard Arkwright (1732–1792) in 1766, was a turning point. Arkwright had originally designed the spinners to be turned by horsepower. Then in 1771 he adapted the machine to run on water power, which is why it came to be called the water frame.

Key Dates

- 1698 Thomas Savery invents the first practical steam engine.

- 1722 Thomas Newcomen improves the steam engine.

- 1733 John Kay invents the flying shuttle weaving machine.

- 1764 James Hargreaves invents the spinning jenny to spin yarn.

- 1766 Richard Arkwright invents the water frame for spinning by water power.

- 1782 James Watt creates a cheap-to-run steam engine for powering machines.

- 1794 Eli Whitney patents his cotton gin, for removing seeds from cotton.

The Charged World

I T WOULD BE HARD TO IMAGINE a world without electricity. Not only is it the energy that powers everything from toasters to televisions, but it is one of the fundamental forces in the Universe, holding all matter together. Yet until the late 18th century, scientists knew almost nothing about electricity. The ancient Greeks knew that when you rubbed a kind of resin called amber with cloth it attracts fluff. The word "electricity" comes from *elektron*, the Greek word for amber. For thousands of years amber attraction was considered a minor curiosity.

In the 18th century scientists such as the French chemist Charles Dufay (1698–1739) and the English physicist Stephen Gray (1666–1736) began to investigate electricity. They soon discovered not only that various substances could conduct (transmit) the same attraction to fluff as amber, but also that rubbing two similar substances together made them repel, not attract, each other. This attraction and repulsion came to be called positive and negative electrical "charge."

▶ THE DYNAMO
The discovery of the link between electricity and magnetism led to the development of the dynamo. It could generate electricity by turning magnets between electrical coils. In 1873 the Belgian Zénobe Gramme built the first practical generator. By 1882 power stations were supplying electric power to both New York and London.

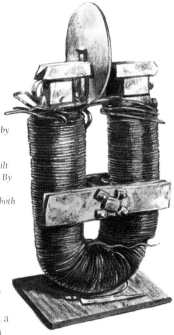

By the mid-1700s some machines could generate quite large charges when a handle was turned to rub glass on sulfur. The charge could even be stored in a special glass jar called a Leyden jar—then suddenly let out via a metal chain to create a spark. Seeing these sparks, the American statesman and inventor Benjamin Franklin (1706–1790) wondered if they were the same as lightning. He attached a metal chain like that of a Leyden jar to a kite sent up in a thunderstorm. The lightning sent a spark from the chain—only much bigger than expected; and Franklin was lucky to survive.

ELECTRICAL PROGRESS

Faraday's and Henry's discovery of a way to generate electricity may have transformed our lives more than any other single scientific discovery. For thousands of years, people had seen at night by candlelight, kept in touch with messages carried on foot or horseback, and heard music only when someone played an instrument near them. The discovery of electricity changed all this.

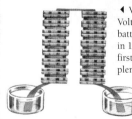

◀ VOLTAIC PILE
Volta's pile, or battery, was invented in 1800. It was the first source of plentiful electricity.

▲ EDISON'S PHONOGRAPH
The first record player, Edison's phonograph of 1877, was mechanical. The arrival of electrical sound recording in the 1920s, including sound on TV and film, made sound and music more accessible.

▲ EDISON'S ELECTRIC LIGHTBULB
The electric lightbulb was invented independently by Sir Joseph Swan, in Britain, in 1878 and by Thomas Edison in the United States, in 1879.

▶ FARADAY AT WORK
Michael Faraday spent his life working at the Royal Institution in London, where his exciting and brilliantly clear public demonstrations of the latest electrical discoveries were famous. For one show he built a big metal cage. He stepped inside it with his instruments, while his assistant charged up the cage to 100,000 volts —a terrifying crackle of sparks ran around it. Faraday knew that he would be safe inside the cage because the charge courses around the outside. Such electrically safe cocoons are now called Faraday cages.

People were so excited by Franklin's discovery that demonstrations of electrical effects became very fashionable. When Italian anatomist Luigi Galvani (1737–1798) found that a dead frog's legs hung on a railing twitched in a thunderstorm, people wondered if they had found the very force of life itself—animal electricity. Alessandro Volta (1745–1827) realized that it was not a "life force" that made the electricity that twitched the frog's legs, but simply a chemical in the metal railing. Soon scientists realized that an electrical charge could be made to flow in a circular path from one side, or "terminal," of a battery to the other.

The real breakthrough, however, was the discovery of the link between electricity and magnetism. In 1819, Danish physicist Hans Øersted suggested that an electrical current has a magnetic effect, turning the needle of a compass. Little more than a decade later Joseph Henry (1797–1878) in the United States and Michael Faraday (1791–1867) in Britain proved that the opposite is, in fact, true—that it is actually a magnet that has an electrical effect. When a magnet is moved near an electric circuit, it generates a surge of electricity in the circuit. Using this principle—called electromagnetic induction—huge machines could be built to generate large quantities of electricity. The way was now open for the development of every modern appliance from electric lighting to the Internet.

▲ ALEXANDER GRAHAM BELL
Bell (1847–1922) was the Scottish-born American inventor of the telephone and a pioneer of sound recording.

▼ THE FIRST TELEPHONE
When Alexander Bell invented the telephone in 1876, electric telegraphs were already widely used to send messages along an electric cable, simply by switching the current on and off. Bell found a way of carrying the vibrations of the voice in a similar electric signal.

Key Dates

- 250 B.C. Parthians invent the battery.
- 1710s Stephen Gray transmits electricity 328 feet along a silk thread.
- 1752 Benjamin Franklin shows that lightning is electricity.
- 1800 Alessandro Volta makes the first modern battery.
- 1819 Hans Øersted discovers that an electric current creates a magnetic field.
- 1820 Georg Ohm shows that the flow of an electric current depends on the resistance of a wire.
- 1830 Joseph Henry and Michael Faraday discover how an electrical current can be generated by magnetism.

Steam Power

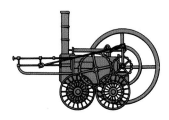

▲ TREVITHICK'S STEAM
LOCOMOTIVE
*The age of modern powered land
transportation began in 1804 with
Trevithick's locomotive, the world's
first steam railroad locomotive. It
ran on a mine track in Wales.*

FOR TENS OF thousands of years, human beings had managed with the power provided by wind, water, or sheer muscle. Then with the Industrial Revolution of the 18th century came the first steam engines, bringing huge amounts of controllable, and reliable, power.

The idea of using steam for power dates back to the 1st century A.D., to an ancient Greek mathematician named Hero, from Alexandria in Egypt. He came up with the idea of using jets of steam to rotate a kettle-like vessel. However, it was not until the 18th century that steam engines became a practical reality.

Most of the early steam engines, including those built by James Watt, were fixed engines, which provided power for working machines and pumps in factories and mines. Then in 1769 a

French army engineer named Nicolas-Joseph Cugnot (1725–1804) built a massive three-wheeled cart that was driven along by a steam engine at walking pace.

The problem with using steam to drive vehicles such as this was that steam engines were incredibly heavy. Weight, though, would not be a problem in boats. In 1783 the Marquis Claude de Jouffroy d'Abbans, a French nobleman, built a steamboat which churned up the Saone River near Lyons, in France, for 15 minutes before the pounding of the engines shook it to bits. The boat sailed only once, but in 1787 John Fitch, an American inventor, made the first successful steamboat with an engine driving a

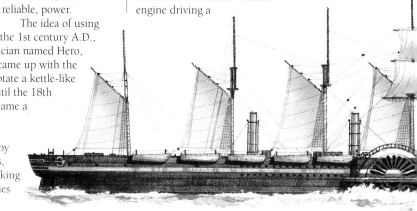

▲ THE ROCKET
In Stephenson's famous *Rocket*, the cylinder that drove the wheels was almost horizontal. This made it so powerful that it easily won the first locomotive speed trials in 1829.

THE FIRST PASSENGER RAILROADS
The first steam locomotives were built to haul coal trucks around mines. On September 27, 1825, a father and son, George and Robert Stephenson, ran the first passenger train from Darlington to Stockton in the north of England. More than 450 people rode in the train's open wagons that day, pulled by the Stephensons' locomotive *Active* (later renamed *Locomotion*), and the 8-mile journey was completed in just 30 minutes. The railroad age had begun.

▲ THE LIVERPOOL AND MANCHESTER
The 40-mile-long Liverpool and Manchester railway, which opened on September 15, 1830, was the first real passenger railroad. On the opening day, it also claimed the first railroad casualty: Home Secretary William Huskisson was killed under the wheels of a locomotive.

series of paddles on each side of the boat. In 1790 Fitch started the world's first steam service on the Delaware River. In 1802, in Scotland, another steam pioneer, William Symington (1763–1831), built a steam tug, the *Charlotte Dundas*. It was so powerful that it could pull two 70-ton barges.

The steamboat really arrived when American engineer Robert Fulton (1765–1815) made the first successful passenger steamboats in 1807. They carried people 150 miles up the Hudson River between New York City and Albany. This journey, which took four days by sailing ship, took Fulton's steamboats less than a day.

Three years earlier, British engineer Richard Trevithick had shown that heavy steam vehicles—or "locomotives" —could move more easily on rails. In 1804 he fired up the world's first steam railroad locomotive, in Wales.

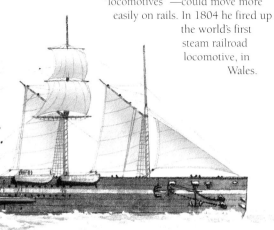

Even rails did not solve the problem at once, because Trevithick's locomotive cracked the cast-iron tracks. But cast-iron rails were soon replaced with wrought-iron and, later, steel rails, which could take more weight. Within 15 years steam locomotives were running on short railroads all over Britain. In 1831 the first regular steam railroad service in the U.S. began, in South Carolina. The age of steam travel had begun.

▲ H.M.S. *THESEUS*
Steamships gained in power and reliability, and in the 1880s many navies began to build steam-power warships like H.M.S. Theseus.

◀ *THE GREAT EASTERN*
In 1819 the New York-built Savannah, *a sailing ship equipped with a steam engine, made the first Atlantic crossing using steam power. The age of regular transatlantic steam passenger services began in 1837 with the launch of the* Great Western, *one of three giant steamships designed by British engineer Isambard Kingdom Brunel. Brunel's* Great Eastern, *launched in 1858, was the biggest ship launched in the 1800s—692 feet long and weighing almost 19,000 tons.*

▶ STEAM SPEED
Steam locomotives were the cutting edge of technology in Victorian Britain. Brilliant men such as James Nasmyth (1808–1890) went into locomotive design in the same way that talented designers are now drawn into electronic and space technology. As a result, steam locomotives rapidly became more and more efficient.

In the U.S., railroads helped to open up the West, cutting journeys of weeks down to a few days. Safety features, such as George Westinghouse's air brake (1872), brought greater speeds —by the 1880s, up to 60mph.

Key Dates

- 1783 Claude d'Abbans sails the first steamboat on the Saone near Lyons, in France.

- 1804 Richard Trevithick builds first steam-powered railroad locomotive.

- 1807 Robert Fulton opens the first passenger steamboat service.

- 1819 The *Savannah* makes the first steam-powered crossing of the Atlantic.

- 1823 George and Robert Stephenson begin to build railroad locomotives.

- 1825 Stockton and Darlington railroad opens in England.

- 1869 The first transcontinental railroad in the United States is completed.

The Story of Life

▲ CHARLES DARWIN
Charles Darwin (1809–1882) was one of the most influential scientists of his day. His theory of evolution is one of the most important ever scientific breakthroughs.

IN THE 18TH CENTURY travelers returning to Europe brought news of thousands of previously unknown plants and animals which they had found on their travels around the world. To try to make sense of these finds, the great Swedish botanist Carl Linnaeus (1707–1778) devised a system of classifying plants and animals into the many species and genera (groups of species) that we still use today.

People began to wonder how all this variety of life had come to be. Perhaps the variety had developed, little by little, over time; but how did this gradual development, or evolution, work? How did new species appear? In 1808 a French naturalist named Jean Lamarck suggested that it happened because animals can change during their lives. For example, organs and muscles that are used a lot become stronger. In this way useful developments are then passed on to an animal's offspring. This was the first proper theory of evolution, but few people were convinced, for they could see that strong parents could produce weak offspring.

▼ DINOSAUR SKELETON
Darwin's theory of evolution arose partly from the first discovery in the 1820s and 1830s of the fossilized bones of huge extinct reptiles which came to be called dinosaurs. In 1824, William Buckland found the jaw of Megalosaurus. The following year, Gideon Mantell found a giant tooth of a creature he called Iguanodon. Soon many more dinosaur fossils were found.

DARWIN'S THEORY
Darwin's theory depends on the fact that no two living things are alike. Some may start life with features that make them better able to survive. For example, an animal might have long legs to help it escape predators. Individuals with such valuable features have a better chance of surviving and having offspring that inherit these features. Slowly, over many generations, better-adapted animals and plants survive and flourish, while others die out or find a new home. In this way, all the millions of species that we know about today gradually evolved.

▼ THE EVOLUTION OF THE HORSE
Species may die out, but they leave behind similar but better-adapted offspring species. The earliest horse, called Eohippus or "dawn horse," was tiny—only 10–20 inches high at the shoulder—and had four toes on each of its front feet. Fossils have shown that a chain of about 30 species, spread over 60 million years, led step by step from Eohippus to the modern horse. Each species is slightly bigger and has fewer toes than its ancestors.

Hyracotherium

Mesohippus

Merychipps

Equus

In the 1820s and 1830s geologists and naturalists made a series of discoveries that were to pave the way for a new theory of evolution, proposed by Charles Darwin. Geologists discovered that the Earth was much older than had previously been thought, and that the landscape of today has evolved over millions of years. At the same time, naturalists discovered more fossils of long-dead creatures, including dinosaurs, showing that many more species had once lived on Earth than are alive today.

Charles Darwin made a long trip around the world on a ship called the *Beagle*, on which he was employed as a botanist. He began to develop a theory of evolution that depended on species' developing as gradually as the landscape. He found an explanation for how this happened in the ideas of the economist Thomas Malthus, who suggested that when populations grow too big for the available resources the weak slowly die out. In the same way, Darwin suggested, species slowly

▲ THE VOYAGE OF THE *BEAGLE*
Between 1831 and 1836, Darwin traveled aboard H.M.S. Beagle as it voyaged around the world on a scientific expedition. He studied plants and animals everywhere the ship landed, including on the Galapagos Islands in the Pacific. While Darwin was sorting through the material that he brought back, he developed the idea of evolution.

◀ UNIQUE WILDLIFE
This is a giant tortoise that lives on the Galapagos Islands ("Galapagos" means "giant tortoise"). Here Darwin found wildlife unique to the islands.

evolve by natural selection as they compete for limited resources—with only the fittest surviving.

The English naturalist Alfred Wallace (1823–1913) independently proposed a theory of evolution similar to Darwin's, and they published their ideas jointly in 1858. It was Darwin's research that gave the theory substance, which is why it is called Darwin's theory. Many people were shocked by Darwin's ideas, but his evidence was hard to ignore, and his theory gradually gained acceptance. Most scientists today see it as one of the greatest-ever scientific breakthroughs.

These finches have longer, thinner beaks for catching insects.

These finches have short, stout beaks for cracking seeds. The bird on the right, has evolved a slightly longer beak as it eats both insects and seeds.

▲ THE GALAPAGOS FINCHES
When Darwin landed in the Galapagos Islands in the Pacific he found slightly different species of finch on each island. These small but significant variations made it clear to Darwin that species must gradually change through time. He thought that species changed in different ways in different places, even if they start the same.

Key Dates

- 1735 Carl Linnaeus groups plants into different species, and subgroups.
- 1788 James Hutton realizes that the Earth is many millions of years old.
- 1801 Jean Lamarck proposes that animal species evolve in response to their habitat.
- 1820s William Buckland and Gideon Mantell discover the first fossils of dinosaurs.
- 1830 Charles Lyell's *Principles of Natural Geology* shows that landscapes evolved gradually.
- 1858 Charles Darwin and Alfred Wallace suggest the theory of evolution by natural selection.

On the Road

▲ THE MODEL T
Cars were toys for the rich in the early days. Then the age of mass motoring dawned in 1908, when Henry Ford launched the Model T Ford, the world's first mass-produced car. By assembling the car from standardized parts on a moving production line, Ford workers could make a Model T so cheaply that people barely able to afford a horse and buggy could easily buy a car. Within five years, 250,000 Americans owned a Model T.

THE STORY OF THE automobile really began in the summer of 1862, when Frenchman Étienne Lenoir drove his small self-propelled cart out through the forests of Vincennes, near Paris, with its small engine slowly thumping. Lenoir's was not the first powered car, however. At the Chinese court a Jesuit priest, Padre Verbiest, had built one as long ago as 1672. Nicolas Cugnot built one in 1769, and over the next 100 years there were many others, including Goldsworthy Gurney's steam carriages (1829), which ran between London and Bath. The problem was that all of these vehicles were powered by steam engines, which tended to be either cumbersome or very expensive to make.

Lenoir's breakthrough was to make a neat little engine that worked by internal combustion—that is, by

▲ FIRST CARS
The idea of steam cars seems quaint nowadays, but many of the first successful automobiles were driven by steam. The steam engine was, after all, a tried and tested form of engine.

burning gas inside a cylinder. Lenoir's gas internal combustion engine was much lighter because it needed neither a tank of water nor a bunker of coal. He set up his engine on an old horse cart so that it drove the

HISTORY OF CARS

Cars have come a long way Since the Benz Motorwagen rolled out of the works in 1888. The earliest cars were built one by one for the rich, but the Ford Model T showed that mass production was the way forward. By the 1930s, mass production enabled many ordinary people to afford cars, but the rich still had individually-built beauties. Cars then were designed mostly by experience and trial-and-error. Car design today relies more on the computer.

▲ 1886 DAIMLER
Gottlieb Daimler was one of the pioneers of motoring. Unlike Benz, who set out to build a motor vehicle from scratch, Daimler fitted an engine to a horse carriage. Like many of the first cars, this had wooden-spoked wheels like a horse cart.

▼ 1901 OLDSMOBILE
This was one of the most popular cars of its time. The Oldsmobile was made by the American Ransom Eli Olds (1864–1950). His 1901 Oldsmobile was steered with a tiller like a boat, rather than with a steering wheel. Many early cars used this means of steering.

▲ MORRIS OXFORD
Millions of Americans had their own cars by the 1920s, thanks to Ford. In the rest of the world cars were still costly. Prices did come down, and soon middle-class families were buying modest sedans such as the Austin Ten, the Opel Kadett, and the Morris.

◀ MAN WITH FLAG
After a few early accidents, cars were seen as highly dangerous machines. For 30 years from 1865, the British "Red Flag" Act required motor vehicles to be preceded by a man on foot waving a red flag. It was not until 1896 that this restriction was lifted and the speed limit raised to 12mph. New York had a Red Flag Act until 1901.

wheels via a chain around the axles. Another Frenchman, Alphonse Beau de Rochas, soon improved the efficiency of Lenoir's engine by using an extra movement, or "stroke," of the piston to squeeze the gas before burning it, making a four-stroke engine. Four-stroke engines are the engines still used in most cars today.

A few years later an Austrian named Siegfried Marcus managed to make an internal combustion engine that ran on gasoline instead of gas. His secret was to create a simple but ingenious device called a carburetor, which turned the gasoline into vapor. In 1873, Marcus built what is now thought to be the world's oldest gasoline-engine car.

It had wheels like a cart but a small steering wheel. It looked more like a car than a horse cart with an engine.

Despite these successes, gasoline-engine cars were still at the experimental stage. Many people believed that the future of the car lay with tried and tested steam engines. Indeed, the land speed record was broken in 1906 not by a gasoline-engine car but by a steam car, the Stanley Steamer, traveling at an astonishing 128mph! The breakthrough for the gasoline engine came with the three-wheel car developed by German engineer Karl Benz and his wife Berta in the 1880s. In 1888, the Benz Patent-Motorwagen became the first automobile ever made for sale to the public. It was such a success that within a decade the Benz factory in Mannheim was turning out 600 cars a year. The automobile age had begun.

▲ FUTURISTIC CAR
Automobile manufacturers are always trying to improve their cars. Top speed, fuel economy, safety, and good looks are all important factors to consider. Manufacturers need to make a car that balances these elements.

▲ VOLKSWAGEN BEETLE
The biggest-selling car ever, the Volkswagen "Beetle," was developed in Germany in the 1940s as a compact and affordable "people's car,"

▲ MORRIS MINI
The 1959 Mini was the first tiny family car. To save space, its designer Alex Issigonis placed the engine across the car, to drive the front wheels.

▶ MCLAREN F1
Plans for Gordon Murray's McLaren F1—designed to be the ultimate road-going car— were released to the public in March 1989. It has a top speed of 231mph.

Key Dates

- 1672 Padre Verbiest builds the world's first steam carriage in China.

- 1769 Nicolas Cugnot builds a three-wheeled steam carriage.

- 1862 Étienne Lenoir builds the first vehicle powered by an internal combustion engine.

- 1865 Alphonse Beau de Rochas builds first four-stroke internal combustion engine.

- 1873 Siegfried Marcus builds the first gasoline-powered car.

- 1888 Karl Benz builds the world's first gasoline-engine car for sale.

- 1908 Henry Ford launches the first mass-produced car, the Ford Model T.

Off the Ground

▲ ORVILLE WRIGHT
Orville Wright was at the controls of his plane, the Flyer, for the world's first controlled flight. The younger of the two Wright brothers, he was born in 1871, in Dayton, Ohio, and died in 1948.

THERE WAS PROBABLY NEVER a time when people did not look up and long to fly like the birds. In ancient Greece there was a myth about an inventor named Daedalus, who made himself wings of feathers and flew high in the sky. Long after, there were those who believed they could mimic the birds and their flapping wings. In the Middle Ages, many reckless pioneers strapped on wings and launched themselves over cliffs and from high towers— only to plummet to the ground.

In the 15th century the brilliant Italian artist and thinker Leonardo da Vinci designed a flying machine with pedal-power wings, which he called an "ornithopter." It was never built and would never have flown, because it was far too heavy. Men did get off the ground every now and then. In ancient China, over 3,000 years ago, the military lifted lookouts aloft on giant kites.

In 1783 two men were carried high in the air over Paris in a giant paper balloon made by the Montgolfier brothers. It was filled with hot air, which rises because it is less dense than cold air. Both kites and balloons were at the mercy of the wind, however, and many inventors believed the future of flight lay with wings.

The great pioneer of winged flight was the British engineer George Cayley (1773–1857). After a series of experiments with kites, Cayley worked out that a wing lifts because its curved upper side boosts air pressure underneath and reduces it above. All modern airplanes are based on the kite-like model glider Cayley built in 1804, with its up-angled front wing and stabilizing tail. In 1853, at the age of 80, he built a full-size glider which is said to have carried his terrified coachman through the air for several hundred yards.

After Cayley, various experimenters tried their luck with gliders. No one

▶ THE WRIGHT BROTHERS' FIRST FLIGHT
One of the secrets of the Wright brothers' success at Kitty Hawk was their development of a way to stop the plane from rolling from side to side—something that had proved the downfall of many earlier planes. Their Flyer had wires to "warp," or twist, the wings to lift one side or the other. This meant that it could not only fly level but also make balanced, banked turns.

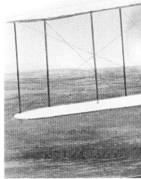

FLYING AHEAD
When Wilbur Wright took their plane, the *Flyer*, to France in 1908, it was clear that the Wrights were far head of pioneers in Europe, such as Louis Blériot. Before long, airplanes were making rapid progress everywhere. On July 25, 1909, Blériot flew across the English Channel. The military demands of World War 1, which began in 1914, gave a tremendous boost to aircraft development. By the time the war was over in 1918, airplanes were reliable enough for the first regular passenger flights to begin.

▶ FIRST HANG-GLIDER
The Wright brothers' ideas on control in flight were preceded in the 1890s by Otto Lilienthal's pioneering flights with craft such as hang gliders. Sadly, Lilienthal was killed flying in 1896.

▲ 1917 BIPLANE
The fighter aircraft of World War I were incredibly flimsy machines, made of fabric stretched over a wooden frame. Most were biplanes— they had two sets of wings—because single wings were far too fragile.

▲ JUMBO JET
The age of mass air travel began with the first jet airliner, the Comet 4, in 1952. Now millions of people fly each year in giant jets such as the Boeing 747 jumbo jet. These planes fly high above the clouds and winds so that the journey is smooth and comfortable.

had any idea how to control their craft in the air until, in the 1890s, a brave young German named Otto Lilienthal built a series of fragile gliders somewhat like modern hang gliders. He succeeded in making the world's first controlled flights in them.

With a glider, a person could fly on wings at last, but not for long. What was needed for sustained flight was an engine. As long ago as 1845 two Englishmen, William Henson and John Stringfellow, built a working model of a plane powered by a lightweight steam engine, which may well have made a successful trial

flight. Steam engines were too weak or too heavy, however, and it was the development of the gasoline engine that proved to be the breakthrough. Even with a gasoline engine, a single wing did not provide enough lift, so experimenters tried adding more and more wings.

Then, one cold Thursday in December 1903 at Kitty Hawk, North Carolina, a gasoline-engine, biplane (double-winged) flying machine built by the brothers Orville and Wilbur Wright rose shakily into the air. It flew 131 feet and then landed safely. It was the world's first controlled, powered, sustained flight.

▼ CONCORDE
By the time the Anglo-French Concorde was built in the 1960s, millions of people were being zoomed around the world each year in high-speed jet airliners. Concorde remains the only successful airliner to carry passengers at supersonic speeds—that is, well above the speed of sound.

▶ STEALTH BOMBER
In 1988, after years of secret development, the U.S. Air Force unveiled its B-2 "stealth" bomber—the most advanced military plane in the world at the time. This sinister-looking aircraft is designed to fly at incredibly high speeds at low altitudes—and be almost invisible to enemy radar. A few years later, it was joined by the F-117 "stealth" fighter. Stealth bombers were used heavily in 1999 in the U.S. bombing raids on Serbia and Kosovo.

Key Dates

- 1783 Two men fly in the Montgolfier brothers' hot-air balloon.

- 1804 George Cayley builds a model kite with wings and a tail.

- 1853 Cayley builds a full-size glider.

- 1890 Clement Ader makes the first powered flight in a steam-powered plane, the *Eole*.

- 1896 Samuel Langley flies about half a mile in his steam-powered *Aerodrome*.

- 1903 Orville and Wilbur Wright make the first controlled, powered flight in the *Flyer*.

- 1909 Louis Blériot flies across the English Channel.

Rays and Radiation

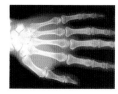

▲ SEE-THROUGH HAND
X-rays can reveal the bones inside a living hand because the rays shine through skin and muscle and are blocked only by bone.

IN 1864 THE SCOTTISH scientist James Clark Maxwell made the brilliant deduction that light is a kind of wave created by the combined effects of electricity and magnetism. He also predicted that light might be just one of many kinds of "electromagnetic" radiation. Scientists were keen to find out, and in 1888 German physicist Heinrich Hertz built a circuit to send big sparks across a gap between two metal balls. If Maxwell was right, the sparks would send out waves of electromagnetic radiation. But they might not be visible like light. So Hertz set up another electric circuit to detect them. The waves created pulses of current in this circuit, which Hertz saw as tiny sparks across another gap. By moving the receiving circuit, he worked out just how long the waves were. They proved to be much longer than light waves; they are now known as radio waves.

About the same time, others were experimenting with discharge tubes. Scientists had known for 100 years or more that a bottle from which air is sucked glows eerily if you put electrodes (electric terminals) into it and fire a spark between them. Discharge tubes gave a near-perfect vacuum (space without air), and the spark between the electrodes made the tube glow brightly. Sometimes even the

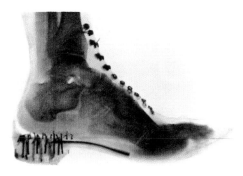

▲ FIRST X-RAY
In 1895, Röntgen shone X-rays through his wife's shoe to make a photo of the bones of her foot inside the shoe.

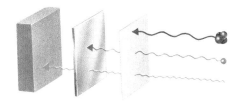

▲ RADIOACTIVITY
We now know that radioactivity is three kinds of particle shot out by atoms as they disintegrate naturally: alpha, beta, and gamma particles. Each kind of particle has the power to penetrate different materials.

THE TV TUBE
The cathode-ray tube did not lead only to the discovery of electrons and radioactivity. Most TV and computer screens are also cathode-ray tubes. The stream of electrons discovered by Thomson is what makes your TV or computer screen glow.

▼ PRISM AND SPECTRUM
In the 1600s Newton showed that light is made of a spectrum, or range, of different colors. We now know that light itself is part of a much wider spectrum of electromagnetic radiation. The radio waves that beam out TV signals are just part of this spectrum.

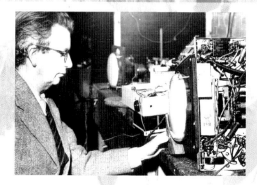

▲ BAIRD'S TELEVISION ATTEMPTS
John Logie Baird (1888–1946) was the Scottish inventor who made television a reality. It had no single inventor, but it was Baird who made the the first true TV pictures in 1926. Baird transmitted TV pictures by telephone line from London to Glasgow in 1928.

▶ THE CURIES IN THEIR LABORATORY
The Curies were among the greatest of all scientific experimenters. Their combination of brilliant insight and exact, patient work led them not only to discover the true nature of radioactivity—radiation from atoms—but to prove it, too.

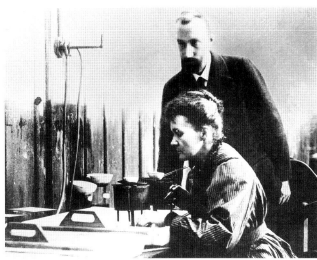

glass glowed. The glowing was named "cathode rays" because it seems to come from the negative terminal, or cathode. If the tube was empty, how was the spark crossing from one electrode to another? In 1897, J. J. Thomson guessed that the spark was a stream of tiny bits of atoms, which he called electrons. For the first time, scientists saw that the atom is not just a solid ball, but contains smaller, subatomic particles.

Meanwhile, in 1895 the discharge tube helped Wilhelm Röntgen to discover another kind of radiation. Röntgen found that, even when passed through thick cardboard, some rays from the tube made a sheet of fluorescent material glow. Although cardboard could block out light it could not stop these new mystery rays, which he called X-rays. He went on to take a picture of the bones in his wife's foot by shining X-rays through it and onto a photographic plate.

In the same year French scientist Henri Poincaré was wondering why the glass in discharge tubes often glowed, as well as the sparks. Perhaps radiation might be emitted not only by electricity but by certain substances, too. Soon, Antoine Becquerel discovered this when he left uranium salts in a dark drawer on photographic paper. A few weeks later there was a perfect image of a copper cross that had

been lying on the paper. There was no light or electricity to form the image, so where was the radiation coming from?

Marie and Pierre Curie soon found that the intensity of radiation was in exact proportion to the amount of uranium. They realized that it must be coming from the uranium atoms themselves, and called this atomic radiation "radioactivity." In fact, not only uranium but also many other elements are radioactive, including two new elements discovered by the Curies—radium and polonium. Since this crucial discovery, many uses for radioactivity have been found, but so too have its dangers. Marie Curie herself died of cancer brought on by overexposure to radioactivity.

▲ BAIRD'S SPINNING DISK
Modern TVs work by scanning streams of electrons back and forth inside a cathode-ray tube. Baird's system was entirely mechanical, using a rapidly spinning disk drilled with holes. The holes let different parts of the picture shine through onto different light-sensitive electric cells.

Key Dates

- 1864 James Clerk Maxwell says that light is electromagnetic radiation.
- 1888 Heinrich Hertz discovers radio waves.
- 1895 Wilhelm Röntgen discovers X-rays.
- 1897 J. J. Thomson discovers electrons.
- 1897 Antoine Becquerel discovers radioactivity.
- 1898 Marie and Pierre Curie discover the radioactive elements radium and polonium.
- 1898–1900 Ernest Rutherford finds that radioactivity is emissions of alpha, beta, and gamma particles.

Space and Time

▲ MICHELSON
Albert Michelson (1852-1931) became the first American scientist to win the Nobel Prize in 1907.

I N 1905, A TALENTED YOUNG scientist named Albert Einstein came up with his special theory of relativity. The theory is not easy to understand, but it has revolutionized the way in which scientists think about space and time. Its origins date back to 1610, when Galileo was thinking about how things moved and described a ship at sea. Shut yourself in a cabin with a tank containing fish, suggested Galileo, and you will see that the fish swim in all directions just as easily when the ship is moving as when it is at anchor. For the fish, the ship's motion is irrelevant. In the same way, when you walk around, you are never aware that the ground beneath your feet is a planet whizzing through space at 62,000mph. So we can detect movement through space only in relation to something else.

Half a century later, a Dutch astronomer named Owe Roemer added another dimension to the picture—time. Roemer realized that because the light from Jupiter took ten minutes to travel across space to the Earth, he was seeing the eclipse of Jupiter's moons, in 1676, ten minutes

▲ EINSTEIN AND E=MC²
Einstein's theory of relativity is not just about space and time; it involves energy too. Energy is how vigorously something can move. Something moving fast clearly has a lot of energy, called kinetic energy. The energy of a heavy ball perched on a hilltop is called potential energy. Scientists knew that kinetic and potential energy are interchangeable—the ball might roll downhill, for example.

Einstein went further and showed that mass, energy, and movement are interchangeable. They are swapping over all the time—energy into mass, mass into movement, and so on. Since light is the fastest moving thing, it clearly plays an important role in the relationship between energy, mass, and movement. Einstein linked them in a famous equation: energy equals mass times the speed of light squared, or $E=mc^2$. This equation shows how a very little mass can give an enormous amount of energy.

TIME MACHINES
Ever since people realized, earlier this century, that time is just a dimension, many have fantasized about the possibility of traveling backward or forward in time. Stories such as H. G. Wells's *The Time Machine* and films such as the *Back to the Future* series center on amazing time machines that can whisk you millions of years into the past or the future, or in some cases just a few minutes or days. Scientists are now beginning to think these may not be just pure fantasies. If time is just another dimension, like length and breadth, what is to stop us from traveling in time to visit the past or the future, just as we travel through space? Einstein himself said it was impossible, and though some scientists think we could do it by bending space–time in some way, no one has yet come up with any convincing ideas of just how it might be possible.

◀ DOCTOR WHO'S TARDIS
The popular British television series Doctor Who had the time-traveling Doctor moving around time and space in his TARDIS, which was disguised as a police phone booth. TARDIS stands for "Time And Relative Dimensions In Space." The TARDIS is remarkable because it warps space and time and because it is many times larger inside than it appears to be on the outside.

▶ THE FOURTH DIMENSION

Einstein's proof that everything is relative upsets our commonsense idea of time. We see time passing as one thing happening after another—as the hands tick around on a clock. It seems that time can move in only one direction, from past to future. But many laws in science, such as Newton's laws of motion, work just as well whether time goes backward or forward. In theory, time could run backward just like a video replay. Einstein's theory showed that this is not just theory, but reality. Many scientists now prefer to think of time, not as a one-way train, but as a dimension, like length, depth, and breadth. The three space dimensions—length, breadth, and depth—combine with the time dimension to make the fourth dimension of space–time.

after it actually occurred. In the same way, when we see a star four million light-years away, we see it as it was four million years ago. Someone elsewhere in the Universe would see the eclipse at a different time. So the timing of events depends on where you are. If this is true, how do you know which is the right time? Is it the time you set on your watch, or the time your friend on a distant planet sets? The fact is, you do not know. You can tell the time only in relation to something else, such as the position of the Sun in the sky or the position of a distant star.

Despite this, 120 years ago most people were sure that behind all this relative time and space there was real, or "absolute," time and real movement. In 1887, two American scientists, A. A. Michelson and E. W. Morley, set out to prove it with an ingenious experiment. They reasoned that a beam of light moving the same way as the

Earth should whizz along slightly slower than one shooting past the opposite way—just as an overtaking bike passes you more slowly than one coming toward you at the same speed. So, they tried to measure the speed of light in different directions. Any difference would show that the Earth was moving absolutely. Yet they detected no difference in the speed of light, in whichever direction they measured it.

Einstein then came to a startling conclusion, which he published as his theory of special relativity. It demolished the idea of absolute time and space forever. Einstein showed not only that light is the fastest thing in the Universe—but that it always passes you at the same speed, no matter where you are or how fast you are going. You can never catch up with a beam of light. Einstein realized that every measurement must be relative, because not even light can help to give an absolute measurement.

◀ KILLING YOUR GRANDPARENTS
A famous argument against the possibility of time travel is about killing your grandparents. The argument asks, what if you traveled back in time to before your parents were born and killed your grandparents? Then neither your parents nor you could have been born. But if you were never born, who killed your grandparents? This kind of problem is called a paradox. Some scientists get around it with the idea of parallel universes, different versions of history that all exist at the same time, running in parallel.

Key Dates

- 1610 Galileo suggests the idea of relative motion.
- 1676 Owe Roemer realizes that light takes time to reach us across space.
- 1887 Michelson and Morley show that the speed of light is the same in all directions.
- 1900 Max Planck invents quantum theory to explain why radiation varies in steps rather than continuously.
- 1905 Albert Einstein publishes his special theory of relativity.
- 1915 Einstein publishes his general theory of relativity.

The Big Universe

▲ EDWIN HUBBLE
Hubble (1889–1953) was an exceptional man. He had trained at Chicago and Oxford in law, and then taken up professional boxing, before turning to astronomy.

Up until the 20th century, astronomers thought the Universe was little bigger than our own Milky Way Galaxy, with the Sun at its center. All the Universe consisted of, they thought, were the few hundred thousand stars they could see with the most powerful telescopes of the day. The largest estimates put the Universe at no more than a few thousand light-years across (one light-year is 5,876 billion miles, the distance light travels in a year). There were fuzzy spiral patches of light they could see through telescopes, but these were thought to be clouds of some kind. They were called spiral nebulae, from the Greek word for "cloud."

In 1918 an American astronomer named Harlow Shapley made an astonishing discovery. Shapley was working at the Mount Wilson Observatory near Los Angeles. He was studying ball-shaped clusters of stars called globular clusters through the observatory's powerful telescope. He wondered why they seemed to be concentrated in one half of the sky and guessed that this is because the Earth is not at the center of the

Galaxy, as had been thought—but right out at the edge, looking inward. He also realized that if this is so, then the Galaxy must be much, much bigger than anyone thought—perhaps as big as 100,000 light-years across.

The discoveries that we are not at the center of the Galaxy but at the edge and that the Galaxy is gigantic were in some ways as dramatic as Copernicus's discovery that the Earth is not at the center of the Solar System. Even as Shapley was publishing his ideas, a new and even more powerful telescope was being installed at Mount Wilson. It enabled a young

▲ THE ANDROMEDA GALAXY
The Andromeda Galaxy is the nearest galaxy beyond our own, and the only one visible with the naked eye. But as Hubble's study of Cepheid variable stars within it showed, even this nearby galaxy is over two million light-years away. Thousands of other galaxies, which are visible only through powerful telescopes, are many billions of light-years away.

BIG BANG

Hubble's discovery that the Universe is getting bigger led to an amazing theory about the history of the Universe. If the Universe is expanding as Hubble showed, it must have been smaller at one time. Indeed, all the signs are that it was once very, very small indeed—perhaps smaller than an atom. The Universe began with an unimaginably gigantic explosion called the Big Bang. It was so big that the galaxies are still being flung out from it today.

◀ THE AFTERGLOW OF THE BIG BANG
The Big Bang theory seemed a very good explanation of the way the Universe is expanding. But there was little real proof until 1992, when the Cosmic Background Explorer (COBE) took a picture of the whole sky showing the microwave radiation coming toward us from all over space. This radiation is the afterglow of the Big Bang, and the slightly uneven pattern shown by the COBE picture confirmed astronomers' theories. Without this unevenness the galaxies could never have formed, so the Big Bang theory would not be correct.

▶ THE STORY OF THE UNIVERSE
By calculating back from the speed of the galaxies, we can estimate that the universe began about 14 billion years ago. Gradually, astronomers have been piecing together the history of the Universe, from the time the first stars and galaxies formed, perhaps 13 billion years ago, through the beginnings of the Earth 4,567,000,000 years ago, the beginning of life some 3,500,000,000 years ago, and the age of the dinosaurs 210–65,000,000 years ago, down to the modern age.

astronomer named Edwin Hubble to make even more astonishing discoveries.

Using the new telescope, Hubble began to look at the spiral nebulae—in particular the nebulae we now know as the Andromeda Galaxy. He could see that it was much more than a fuzzy patch of light and actually contained stars. Among these stars he could see special stars called Cepheid variables, which are so predictable in their brightness that we can use them as distance markers in the sky. The Cepheid variables showed Hubble that Andromeda is several hundred thousand light-years away—far beyond the edge of the Galaxy.

Soon it became clear that many of the fuzzy patches of light in the night sky were other galaxies of stars, even farther away. Suddenly the Universe seemed much, much bigger than anyone had dreamed of. In 1927 Hubble made an even more amazing discovery. While studying the light from 18 galaxies,

he noticed that the light from each one had a slightly different red tinge. He realized that this was because the galaxies are zooming away from us so fast that light waves are actually stretched out and become redder. Remarkably, the farther away the galaxies are, the faster they seem to be moving away from us. Hubble realized that this is because the Universe is expanding.

So within ten years the Universe, which was thought to be just a few thousand light-years across, was found to be many millions, and it was known to be growing bigger at an absolutely astonishing rate. Astronomers can now see galaxies 13 billion light-years away—zooming away from us at nearly the speed of sound.

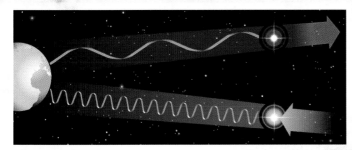

▲ RED SHIFT
We know galaxies are speeding away from us because their light is "red-shifted." If a light source is rushing away, each light wave is sent from a little farther on—and so gets stretched out. As the light waves are stretched out, the light appears redder. The most distant galaxies have such huge red shifts that they must be moving very, very fast. Red shift is based on the observation by Austrian physicist Christian Doppler (1803–1853) that sound waves moving away are stretched out in the same way. The roar of a train coming toward you is high-pitched. As it zooms on past and away, the pitch drops as the sound waves become longer.

Key Dates

- 1918 Harlow Shapley shows that Earth is on the edge of the Galaxy.

- 1929 Hubble shows that Andromeda is a galaxy beyond our own.

- 1927 Hubble realizes that other galaxies are flying away from us—and the Universe is expanding.

- 1927 Abbé George Lemaitre proposes that the Universe began in a Big Bang.

- 1948 Alpher and Herman suggest that the Big Bang left behind weak radiation.

- 1964 Penzias and Wilson detect weak cosmic background radiation, providing evidence for the Big Bang.

Miracle Cures

▲ ALEXANDER
FLEMING
*The discovery of penicillin,
the first antibiotic, by
Scottish bacteriologist
Alexander Fleming (1881–
1955) was one of the great
medical breakthroughs of
the 20th century. For the
first time doctors had a
powerful weapon against a
wide range of diseases.*

I N 1900 DISEASE WAS A frighteningly normal part of life—and death. Few large families of children ever grew up without at least one of them dying. The introduction of vaccination began to save many people from catching diseases such as smallpox. Doctors could do very little once anyone actually became ill, except tend them and pray. To catch a disease such as tuberculosis or syphilis was very likely to be a death sentence.

The main reason for doctors' helplessness in the face of infectious (catching) diseases was the fact that they had no idea what caused them. Then, in the late 19th century, thanks to the work of scientists such as Louis Pasteur, it finally became clear that it was tiny, microscopically small germs such as bacteria and viruses that were to blame.

Gradually medical scientists, especially those in Germany, began to realize that it might be possible to fight infectious disease with chemicals that targeted the germs but left the body unharmed. A very dedicated scientist named Paul Ehrlich believed that the key was to find chemical "magic bullets" that could be aimed at

▲ ERNST CHAIN
*Along with Howard Florey, Chain continued the research
into penicillin that had been started by Alexander Fleming.
The value of the three men's work was recognized in 1945
when they were awarded the Nobel Prize for Medicine.*

ANTIBIOTICS
Antibiotics work by attacking germ cells, but not body cells, and they have proved remarkably effective at treating a variety of bacterial diseases, including pneumonia, meningitis, scarlet fever, syphilis, tuberculosis, and other infections. There are at least 70 useful antibiotics. Most are used against bacterial infections, but some attack fungal diseases and a few are designed to work against cancer. Diseases caused by viruses, however, cannot be treated by antibiotics in any way.

▼ HOW ANTIBIOTICS WORK
Antibiotics fight germs in a number of ways. Some antibiotics make the germ cell's skin leak vital nutrients or let in poisonous substances, but they have no affect on human cell skins. Others, such as penicillin, work by stopping the germ cell's tough skin from forming. Human cells do not have the same tough skins, so they are left unharmed. A third kind of antibiotic, including streptomycin and rifampicin, interferes with chemical processes inside the germ cell.

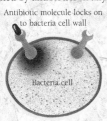

Antibiotic molecule locks on
to bacteria cell wall

Bacteria cell

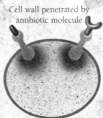

Cell wall penetrated by
antibiotic molecule

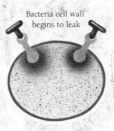

Bacteria cell wall
begins to leak

Bacteria begins
to die

germs. With his colleague Sahachiro Hata, Ehrlich worked to find such a cure for syphilis—a terrible disease that had killed millions of people over the centuries. In 1910 he discovered the chemical arsphenamine, which was later sold under the name Salvarsan. It wiped out the germ that causes syphilis while leaving body cells virtually unharmed.

For the first time, doctors had a powerful weapon against a disease, and the search was now on for similar chemical treatments for other diseases. The early hopes were dashed, and it was not until the 1930s that scientists discovered a group of chemicals named sulfonamides that were deadly to a wide range of bacteria. In the meantime, a British scientist called Alexander Fleming had made a remarkable discovery.

In 1928 Fleming was working in his laboratory in St. Mary's Hospital, London, when he noticed a strange thing. He had been culturing (growing) the staphylococcus bacteria in a dish, and it had grown moldy. What was remarkable was that the bacteria seemed to have died wherever the mold was. Fleming had a hunch that this mold, called *Penicillium notatum*, could be useful against disease.

Fleming himself was unable to find out if his hunch was true, but ten years later Howard Florey, Ernst Chain, and others took up the idea and developed the first antibiotic drug, penicillin. "Antibiotic" means germ-attacking. Penicillin, one of the miracle drugs of the 20th century, has saved many, many millions of people from dying from a wide range of infectious diseases, including tuberculosis. Since then, thousands

▲ CLEAN BILL OF HEALTH
In the 1850s Austrian Ignaz Semmelweiss found that he could save women from dying in childbirth in hospital by getting his medical students to wash their hands to stop the spread of infection. Later, Joseph Lister introduced phenol to kill germs in surgery. These antiseptic (germ-killing) techniques were not miracle cures, but they made hospitals, such as this smallpox hospital, much, much safer.

of other antibiotic drugs have been discovered. In the early 1940s, for instance, the American scientist Selman Waksman found the antibiotic streptomycin in soil fungi. Some antibiotics come from nature, mainly molds and fungi, and some have been made artificially from chemicals. None has proved as effective and safe against such a broad range of diseases as penicillin.

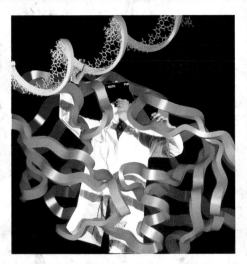

◀ NEW DRUGS
In the past, drugs either occurred naturally or were created in the laboratory. In future, some may be created in cyberspace, as chemists put computer models of molecules together with models of body cells to see how they react, which is what this chemist is doing. Computers may be able to trawl through millions of different ways of putting atoms together very quickly to find the perfect "magic bullet" that targets the disease precisely.

Key Dates

- 1867 Joseph Lister shows the value of antiseptic surgery.

- 1860s Louis Pasteur insists that many diseases are caused by germs.

- 1876 Robert Koch proves that germs can cause disease.

- 1910 Ehrlich and Hata find that Salvarsan is a cure for syphilis.

- 1928 Florey, Chain, and others turn penicillin into the first antibiotic.

- 1942 Waksman discovers streptomycin.

- 1951 Frank Burnet discovers how the immune system attacks germs but not body cells.

Nuclear Power

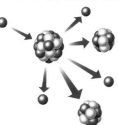

▲ NUCLEAR FISSION
In nuclear fission, an atom is split by the impact of a tiny neutron. As it splits into two smaller atoms, it releases a lot of energy and two more neutrons, which may split more atoms.

No SCIENTIFIC DISCOVERY has been so awesome as that of nuclear energy, the energy in the nucleus of every atom in the Universe. Nuclear energy is not only the energy that makes nuclear weapons, it is the energy that keeps every star in the Universe burning. Until the 20th century, this vast power was undreamed of. Scientists knew that matter was made of atoms, but they thought atoms were no more lively than billiard balls. No one knew what energy really was.

Albert Einstein had a brilliant insight in his theory of special relativity of 1905. He showed that energy and matter are flip sides of the same basic thing, swapping back and forth all the time. His famous equation $E=mc^2$ gave this swap a real quantity. E is energy, and m the mass, or quantity, of matter; c is the speed of light, which is huge. If the mass of a tiny atom could be changed to energy, some scientists believed it would yield a huge amount of power.

At the same time, scientists such as Neils Bohr were probing the atom and finding that it is not just a ball. First, they found that it holds tiny electrons whizzing around a nucleus, or core, of larger

▼ NUCLEAR MUSHROOM
When a nuclear bomb explodes on the ground, a huge fireball vaporizes everything on the ground and turns it into a blast of hot gases and dust that shoots far up into the sky. When this blast reaches the stratosphere, one of the layers of the atmosphere that finishes 50km from the earth's surface, it begins to cool, and some of the gases condense into dust. As the dust begins to fall it billows out in a distinctive mushroom-shaped cloud. Often radioactive particles drop back to the ground.

THE MANHATTAN PROJECT
The bombs dropped on Hiroshima and Nagasaki were developed in a secret program, called the Manhattan Project, by a team at Los Alamos, New Mexico. On July 16, 1945, the Los Alamos team exploded the first atomic bomb in the desert, to the amazement of spectators in bunkers 5 1/2 miles away.

The team achieved the critical mass of fission material (plutonium-239 and uranium-235) in two ways. One was to smash two lumps together from opposite ends of a tube, a system called "Thin Man." The other was to wrap explosive around a ball of fission material and smash it together ("Fat Man"). The Hiroshima bomb was a uranium-235 "Thin Man." The Nagasaki bomb was a plutonium-239 "Fat Man."

▲ J. ROBERT OPPENHEIMER
Oppenheimer (1904–1967) led the Los Alamos team, but he later opposed hydrogen bombs. These are powerful nuclear bombs based not on the fission (splitting) of atoms but on the fusion (joining together) of tiny hydrogen atoms.

▼ NAGASAKI
The effect of the nuclear bombs on Hiroshima and Nagasaki was so terrible that no one has used them in warfare again. The bombs obliterated huge areas of both cities and killed over 100,000 people instantly. Many of those who survived the initial blast died slow and painful deaths from the aftereffects of radiation.

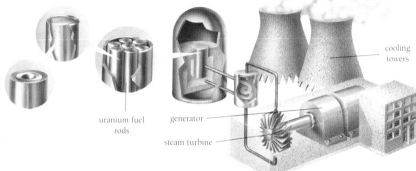

▶ NUCLEAR POWER
A nuclear bomb is an uncontrolled nuclear chain reaction. In a nuclear power plant, the reaction is slowed down and sustained almost indefinitely to provide a huge amount of heat from just a small amount of uranium fuel. This heat boils water to make steam, which drives around the turbines (fan blades) that generate the electricity.

uranium fuel rods

generator

steam turbine

cooling towers

protons. Then, in 1932, James Chadwick discovered a second kind of particle in the nucleus—the neutron.

At once, Italian atomic scientist Enrico Fermi tried firing neutrons at the nuclei of uranium atoms. He found different atoms forming and guessed that the neutrons had joined the uranium atoms to make bigger atoms of an unknown element, which he called element 93. But Fermi was wrong. In 1939, German scientists Otto Hahn and Fritz Strassman repeated Fermi's experiment. What they found was not a new element but something even more astonishing—so astonishing that Hahn hardly dared believe it. It was a woman physicist, Lise Meitner who explained to the world what Fermi, Hahn, and Strassman had done. They had split the uranium atom in two, making smaller atoms including barium. This splitting of the atom is called fission.

When the uranium atom split, it not only released a lot of energy, but also split off two neutrons. What if these two neutrons zoomed off to split two new atoms? These atoms would then, in turn, release two more neutrons, which

would split more atoms, and so on. Scientists soon realized that this could become a rapidly escalating chain reaction of atom splitting. A chain reaction such as this would unleash a huge amount of energy as more and more atoms split.

Normally, chain reactions will not start in uranium because only a few uranium atoms are of the kind that splits easily, namely uranium-235. Most are tougher uranium-238 atoms. To make a bomb or a nuclear power plant, you need to pack enough uranium-235 into a small space to sustain a chain reaction. This is known as the critical mass.

During World War II, scientists in Germany and the United States worked furiously to achieve the critical mass; neither wanted to be last to make the atomic bomb. The Americans realized that another atom—plutonium-239—might be used instead of uranium-235. At 3:45 p.m. on December 2, 1942, a team in Chicago led by Fermi used plutonium-239 to achieve a fission chain reaction for the first time. In August 1945, American fission bombs devastated the Japanese cities of Hiroshima and Nagasaki.

▲ NUCLEAR POWER PLANT
Nuclear reactions release huge amounts of energy, but they create dangerous radioactivity too. Radioactivity can make people very ill or even kill them. Many people suffered radiation sickness after the Hiroshima and Nagasaki bombs. Even nuclear power plants can have dangerous leaks. A serious nuclear accident occurred when the Chernobyl reactor, in the Ukraine, went wrong in April 1986, spreading radioactive material over a vast area. The radioactive material produced by nuclear power plants must be stored safely for hundreds of years until it loses its radioactivity.

Key Dates

- 1905 Einstein reveals the theoretical power of the atom in special relativity.

- 1911 Rutherford proposes that atoms have a nucleus, circled by electrons.

- 1919 Rutherford discovers the proton.

- 1932 Chadwick discovers the neutron.

- 1939 Hahn and Strassman split a uranium atom.

- 1942 Fermi's team achieves the first fission chain reaction.

- 1945 July 16: Oppenheimer's team explodes the first atomic bomb.

- 1945 August: U.S. Air Force drops atomic bombs on Nagasaki and Hiroshima.

Lifeplan

EVERY LIVING THING—EVERY human, animal, and plant—is made up from millions of tiny packages called cells. Inside each cell is a remarkable chemical molecule called DNA. It is the basis of all life. The DNA in human body cells not only tells each cell how to play its part in keeping the body alive but also carries all the instructions for making a new human being. The discovery of DNA's shape by James Watson and Francis Crick in 1953 was one of the major scientific breakthroughs of the 20th century, and the impact of their discovery on our lives has already been huge.

DNA (deoxyribonucleic acid) was discovered in 1869 by a Swiss student named Friedrich Miescher. Miescher was looking at pus on old bandages under a microscope when he saw tiny knots in the nucleus, or core, of

▲ DNA
DNA is one of the largest molecules known, weighing 500 million times more than a molecule of sugar. It is very thin, but very long—if stretched out it would be about 16 inches long. The molecule is usually coiled up, but it is made from two thin strands wrapped around each other in a twin spiral, or "double helix." It is somewhat like a long twisted rope ladder, with rungs made of chemicals called bases.

▲ FAMILY
Everyone has their own unique DNA, and it is so distinctive that it can be used to prove who you are, like a fingerprint. You get half your DNA from your mother and half from your father. There are sequences of bases in your DNA that are so similar to both your mother's and your father's that an analysis of your DNA proves who your parents are. DNA is also the reason why we all bear some resemblance to our parents.

the pus cells. His tutor, Ernst Hoppe-Sayler, analyzed these nuclear knots chemically and found that they were acidic, so they called the substance nucleic acid. No one at the time had much inkling of its real significance.

Seventy-six years later, in 1945, American bacteriologist Oswald Avery was studying influenza bacteria when he noticed that DNA could turn a harmless bacteria into a dangerous one—as if it were giving instructions. In 1952 Alfred Hershey and Martha Chase

THE CHEMICALS OF LIFE
The study of the chemicals of life, such as DNA, is called organic chemistry, or biochemistry. It can also be called carbon chemistry because, remarkably, all life depends on chemicals that include atoms of carbon. There are literally millions of these carbon compounds, because carbon atoms are uniquely able to form links with other atoms. Some, such as proteins and amino acids, are more important than others.

▶ NICOTINE MOLECULE
Many organic compounds are based on a ring, or hexagon, of six carbon atoms. This is a model of the compound nicotine, found in the dried leaves of the tobacco plant. It is a poison used as an insecticide. It is also the chemical in cigarettes that makes people addicted to smoking.

▼ PROTEINS
Proteins are the basic material of all living cells. They are built up from different combinations of chemicals called amino acids. All these amino acids are present in each cell, like these cells from around human teeth. To make a protein, DNA must instruct the cell to make the right combination of amino acids.

showed that this is just what DNA does. Once DNA's importance became clear, the race was on to find out how it worked. It was crucial to discover the shape of this long and complex molecule. In 1952 Rosalind Franklin, a young woman working at Imperial College in London, photographed DNA using X-rays, but she could not figure out its structure. The young American Watson and Englishman Crick were then working on DNA at the Cavendish Laboratory in Cambridge, England. When they saw Rosalind Franklin's photographs, they suddenly realized that the DNA molecule is shaped like a double helix—that is, like a rope ladder twisted in a spiral.

After this great discovery, biochemists began to take DNA apart piece by piece under microscopes, then put it together again to find out how it gave instructions. The search focused on the four different chemicals making up the "rungs" of the ladder: guanine, cytosine, adenine, and thymine. Erwin Chagraff found that these four "bases" pair up only in certain ways—guanine links only with cytosine; adenine only with thymine.

It soon became clear that the key to DNA lies in the order, or sequence, of the bases along each of the molecule's two long strands. Like the bits of a computer, the sequence of bases works as a code. The bases are like letters of the alphabet, and the sequence is broken up into "sentences" called genes. The code in each gene is the cell's instructions to make a particular protein, one of the basic materials of life. The complete gene code, or genetic code, was finally worked out in 1967 by American biochemists Marshall Nirenberg and Indian-American Har Khorana—work that earned them the Nobel Prize.

▲ STAYING ALIVE
Not only humans, but every living thing in the world has a DNA molecule in each of its body cells. This remarkable molecule tells the cell exactly what to do in keeping the living thing's body together, whether it is a bear or a salmon. It is also a complete copy of instructions for making an entirely new bear or salmon.

▲ THE GENETIC CODE
The key to the DNA code lies in the sequence of chemical bases along each strand, shown here in the form of a DNA fingerprint. These bases are a bit like letters of the alphabet, and the sequence is broken up into "sentences" called genes. Each gene provides the instructions to make a particular set of proteins.

Key Dates

- 1869 Miescher discovers DNA.

- 1945 Avery discovers that DNA issues life instructions to living things.

- 1952 Hershey and Chase show that DNA carries genetic instructions.

- 1953 Watson and Crick show that DNA has a double-helix (spiral) structure.

- 1954 Chagraff shows that DNA's four "bases" join together only in certain ways.

- 1961 Brenner and Crick show how so-called "letters" in the DNA code are formed by triplets of bases.

- 1967 Nirenberg and Har Khorana show how the genetic code works.

50

The Power of the Processor

▲ MICROCHIP
Microprocessors are made from thousands of tiny transistors joined in circuits and printed onto a tiny slice of silicon, or silicon chip. The biggest parts of a chip are not its circuits and switches—the tiny patch in the center—but the connecting teeth along its sides.

THE COMPUTER'S ORIGINS date back 5,000 years when people in Asia used abacuses to do sums. An abacus is a simple frame with rows of sliding beads, but a skilled user can do complex computations very quickly. In the 1600s, men such as French mathematician Blaise Pascal, built adding machines with gears and dials.

The first real computer was an "analytic engine" designed in the 1830s by Englishman Charles Babbage along with the poet Byron's daughter Ada Lovelace. This machine would have used cards punched with holes to control the movement of rods and gears, and so make complex calculations. Crude mechanical systems though, were not up to the task, and Babbage never built it.

During the next 100 years, people built increasingly clever calculators using punch cards to control rods and dials. These were just adding machines and could not do the complex sums we expect of a computer. Mechanical devices were too big and noisy. In 1944, Howard Aiken and IBM did build a basic computer using punch cards, but it was over 49 feet long and had less computing power than a modern pocket calculator!

The way forward for computers was to replace mechanics with electronics. Electronics are at the heart of most modern technologies, from CD players to rocket-control systems. They work by using electricity to send signals. Inside every electronic device there are lots of small electric circuits, which continually switch on and off telling the device what to do. Unlike electric light switches on the wall, electronic switches work automatically.

The first electronic device, called a valve, was invented in 1904. It looked like an electric lightbulb and was used in radios and TVs. In 1939 American physicist John Atasanoff built a valve computer at Iowa University. A few years later, during World War II, an English mathematician named Alan Turing developed a giant valve

◀ VIRTUAL REALITY
Virtual reality (VR) systems build a picture electronically to create the impression of a real 3D space. They were developed in the 1960s in simulators that taught jet pilots how to fly. With VR, people can operate a computer-guided device in dangerous or difficult places, for example in an underwater wreck or inside the body.

THE TRANSISTOR
In the 1940s, TVs and other electronic devices relied on huge, hot-running glass tubes (somewhat like lightbulbs) for fine control over electric currents. Then John Bardeen and his colleagues showed that the same control could be achieved with tiny, solid lumps of semiconductor materials—special materials such as germanium and silicon that conduct electricity only when warmed up by another electric current. The development of integrated circuits and microchips, on which all modern electronic technology relies, stems from this discovery.

◀ BARDEEN AND COLLEAGUES
The transistor was created by three scientists working together at the Bell Laboratories in 1948 —John Bardeen, William Shockley, and Walter Brattain.

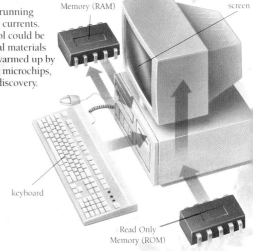

Random Access Memory (RAM)

screen

keyboard

Read Only Memory (ROM)

computer called Colossus to break the secret German "Enigma" codes. Turing also created many of the basic rules of computing. Valves were used in the first electronic computers built for sale in the early 1950s, called first-generation computers. However, the valves were big, got very, very hot, and kept failing.

The big breakthrough came when valves were replaced with transistors. Transistors are switches, like valves, but they are made from special "semiconductor" materials, such as silicon and germanium, which can change their ability to conduct electricity. Transistors are lumps of these material inserted with electrodes (conductors). These can be very small and robust.

With transistors, computers moved on to the second and third generations in the 1950s and 1960s, but they were still small and expensive. Then, in 1958, American Jack Kilby put the connections for two transistors inside one 3/8-inch-long crystal of silicon—he had made the world's first integrated circuit, or microchip.

Soon microchips were getting smaller and smaller, and electronic circuits became increasingly complicated as scientists discovered new ways of squeezing more and more components into a single chip. Nowadays, microchips, or silicon chips, range from simple circuits for electric teakettles to complex

high-speed microprocessors with millions of transistors capable of running computer programs at very high speeds.

With integrated circuits, computers could start to be miniaturized. Heat ceased to be a real problem, and a great deal of computing power could be packed into a tiny space. The first computer based on a microprocessor was the Intel (1974), which moved computers into the fourth and fifth generations. Since then, they have progressed in leaps and bounds in terms of reliability, speed, and power. Today's computers are packed into such compact and inexpensive packages that the average household in most developed countries can now have its own high-powered computer.

◀ COMPUTER GRAPHICS
The sophisticated graphics (pictures) now seen on ordinary home computers require levels of computing power that would have been envied by the scientists guiding spacecraft through the Solar System just 15 years ago. Every computer we use is still built around the microprocessor.

◀ SCREEN AND KEYBOARD
The keyboard and TV-like screen of the computer are so familiar that we take them for granted. Flat screens which are thin enough to hang on the wall have already been developed. So, too, have voice-operating systems that may make the keyboard redundant.

◀ ELEMENTS OF A COMPUTER
Inside a computer are a number of microchips. Some of a computer's memory, called the ROM (read-only memory), is built into these microchips. A computer also has chips for RAM (random-access memory), which takes new data and instructions whenever needed. Data can also be stored on magnetic patterns on removable disks, or on the laser-guided bumps on a CD.

At the heart of every computer is a powerful microchip called the central processing unit (CPU). The CPU is the part that works things out, within guidelines set by the ROM, and processes and controls all the programs by sending data to the right place in the RAM.

▲ TRANSISTOR
The modern computer was born when the transistor was invented in 1948. Modern microprocessors contain millions of transistors packed onto tiny silicon chips, but they still work in the same way as this single transistor.

Key Dates

- 1642 Pascal invents an adding machine.

- 1835 Babbage begins to build his programmable analytic engine.

- 1847 George Boole devises the basis of computer logic.

- 1930 Vannevar Bush builds a mechanical computer.

- 1937 Atsanoff builds a digital electronic computer.

- 1939 Aiken builds a valve computer.

- 1948 Shockley, Bardeen, and Brattain invent the transistor.

- 1958 Jack Kilby invents silicon chip.

Space Age

▲ THE EARTH
FROM SPACE
Viewing the Earth from space has been one of the most extraordinarily powerful experiences of the space age. It makes clear what we had never been able to see before— that the Earth is an almost perfect sphere. It has also made us much more aware of the frailty of our planet.

THE CONQUERING OF SPACE has been one of the great human achievements of the 20th century. What was barely a fantasy 100 years ago is now an everyday reality. Over 100 artificial satellites are launched into space every year, manned space flights are commonplace, and space probes have visited all but one of the planets in the Solar System. The *Mir* space station was recently abandoned after 13 years as an orbiting laboratory in space.

The space age began on October 4, 1957 when the Soviet Union launched *Sputnik* (later called *Sputnik 1*). It was blasted straight up by powerful rockets, and as the rockets fell away *Sputnik* soared on upward, leveled out, and hurtled into the first-ever orbit of the Earth. A month later, the first living creature went into space in *Sputnik 2*—a dog called Laika. Sadly, Laika never came back.

On April 12, 1961, brave Russian cosmonaut Yuri Gagarin went up in *Vostok 1* to become the first man in space. *Vostok 1* took Gagarin once around the Earth before re-entering the atmosphere and parachuting into the ocean. A few months later U.S. astronaut Alan Shepard went up, and in June 1963 Valentina Tereshkova became the first woman in space in *Vostok 6*. In 1965, Russian Alexei Leonov stepped outside a spacecraft in space, floating on the end of a cable.

During the early years of the space age, the United States and Soviet Union were engaged in a bitter rivalry called the Cold War. Each was determined to beat the other in the "space race." Throughout the 1960s and 1970s, each nation was spurred on to ever more spectacular and showy

◀ GAGARIN
Born of a poor Russian farming family, Yuri Gagarin became the most famous person in the world in 1961 when Vostok 1 made him the first man in space. His flight around the Earth lasted just 1 hour 48 minutes, but it was a spectacular moment in human history. Sadly, Gagarin died only seven years later at the age of 34 while testing a new plane.

EXPLORING SPACE
On July 17, 1969, the giant *Saturn V* rocket launched three astronauts toward the Moon on the *Apollo 11* mission. Three days later, the Apollo command module was circling the Moon. While Michael Collins stayed in the command module, Neil Armstrong and Buzz Aldrin went down to the Moon's surface in the lunar module. On July 20, Neil Armstrong opened the hatch and climbed out onto the Moon.

▶ THE LUNAR MODULE
Artmstrong and Aldrin went down to the Moon's surface in the tiny lunar module, which was little bigger than a trailer. When it landed, four legs supported it on big pads on the soft, dusty surface.

▲ FIRST STEPS
Neil Armstrong was the first man on the Moon. As he climbed down the ladder of the lunar module and stepped onto the Moon's surface, he said these now-famous words: "That's one small step for a man, one giant leap for mankind."

▶ MIR
Despite a number of mishaps, the Soviet Mir spacecraft stayed up in space for over 13 years, between 1986 and 1999, and made more than 76,000 orbits of the Earth. It was a temporary home to many astronauts—and Russian Valery Polyakov spent a record 437 continuous days aboard.

achievements. Both the United States and the USSR sent probes to the same planets, including Venus (the American *Mariners* and the Soviet *Veneras*) and Mars. Both sent probes to the Moon. Then, in July 1969, the Americans went ahead by putting men on the Moon. The Soviets could go no better, but within two years they launched *Salyut 1*, the first space station.

Although these achievements were spectacular, the space race cost the two superpowers a fortune, and by the end of the 1970s it began to slow down. Today the Cold War is over, cooperation in space is the spirit of the day, and the Americans and Russians are working with Canada, Europe, and Japan to build a huge international space station (ISO), which is being assembled in space piece by piece.

One cause of controversy among those involved in space exploration has been whether to focus on manned or unmanned exploration. Unmanned probes are cheaper, safer, and faster than manned vehicles and can make trips far too risky for human beings to attempt. No manned probe is ever likely to descend into Saturn's atmosphere or venture out beyond the edge of the Solar System—partly because manned spacecraft must return.

Unmanned probes have already visited most of the Solar System's planets. They have landed on Mars and Venus and they have told us a huge amount about all the planets. Unmanned probes can never give as full a picture as human observers, and cannot react so well to unexpected events. Manned spacecraft have been sent to the Moon, but sending people to the planet Mars is far trickier. Even the journey itself would take many months and would be a tremendous ordeal for astronauts. Most experts think astronauts may land on Mars by 2020.

▲ MARS LANDING
No manned spacecraft has landed on another planet, but many unmanned probes have landed on Mars. In July 1997, the U.S. *Mars Pathfinder* touched down on Mars and beamed back "live" TV pictures from the planet. Two days later, it sent out a wheeled robot vehicle called *Sojourner* to survey the surrounding area.

▼ THE SPACE SHUTTLE
Early spacecraft were usable only for one flight, but the U.S. space shuttle of 1981 was the first reusable craft, landing again with the aid of plane-like wings. It made short flights in space much easier.

Key Dates

- 1957 *Sputnik* is the first spacecraft to orbit the Earth.

- 1957 Laika the dog is the first living creature in space.

- 1961 Yuri Gagarin is the first man in space.

- 1961 Alan Shepard is the first American in space.

- 1963 Valentina Tereshkova is the first womna in space.

- 1965 Alexei Leonov does the first space walk.

- 1969 Neil Armstrong and Buzz Aldrin are the first men to land on the Moon.

Instant Contact

▲ TELEPHONES
Since its invention by Alexander Graham Bell in 1876, the telephone has become a vital part of our lives, giving us the instant contact we now take for granted.

THE AGE OF INSTANT communication began when American painter and inventor Samuel Morse invented the electric telegraph in the 1830s. The telegraph linked two places by electric wire. By simply switching the current rapidly on and off, one could send a message in a code of pulses, called Morse code. For the first time, people could send messages almost instantly over long distances. On May 24, 1844, Morse sent this message from Washington, D.C., to Baltimore over the world's first commercial telegraph line: "What hath God wrought?"

Newspapers quickly began to use the Morse telegraph to send news stories, and by the 1860s the telegraph was the main means of long-distance communication in the United States, linking all major cities. Thanks to the backing of American banker Cyrus W. Field and British physicist Lord Kelvin, a telegraph cable was laid all the way under the Atlantic

in 1866. The benefit was instant. Once, even urgent messages between London and New York had taken weeks to get through. Suddenly, via the transatlantic cable, contact was almost instant.

However, messages still had to be transmitted in an elaborate code. A few years later, in Boston, the Scotsman Alexander Graham Bell found a way to transmit not just single pulses, but multiple pulses down the telegraph wire. In 1875 he found a way to transmit all the vibrations made by sounds as multiple pulses. On March 10, 1876, he transmitted human

▼ THE INVENTION OF RADIO
The telegraph and the telephone rely on a physical connection by wire. In 1895 Guglielmo Marconi transmitted a Morse message across empty space using pulses of radio waves.

INTERNET
The Internet is a vast network linking millions of computers around the world. It transmits huge amounts of information, including words, images, and sounds. It began in the 1960s when the U.S. army developed a network called ARPAnet to link military and government computers in case of nuclear war. Soon places such as universities developed their own networks.

In 1983, the university networks merged with ARPAnet to form the Internet. Now anyone with a computer, a modem, and a phone line can join. Originally the Internet was used just for electronic mail (e-mail) and transferring files. But there was a huge explosion of interest in the Internet after Tim Berners-Lee of the CERN laboratories in Switzerland developed the World Wide Web in 1989 for finding your way around Internet sites.

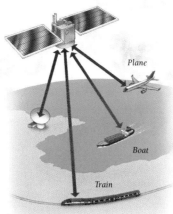

Satellites links will soon connect be able to link you to the internet wherever you are

◀ THE NET
Just as you can talk on the phone, so computers can talk to each other on the Internet. Every computer has its own "address" where it can receive messages, like a telephone number. Computers that have a "site"—a window of information open to all— have a website address, too.

When you access the Net, your computer connects via a local phone line to a big computer called a net provider. This, in turn, is linked to a bigger computer called a main hub. Each main hub is connected to about 100 other main hubs around the world. Some messages travel between main hubs by phone lines and others are linked by satellite. Either way, they are incredibly fast and are called "fast-truck connections."

speech for the first time, saying to his colleague in another room: "Watson, come here. I want you!" By the end of the 19th century every major city in the world was linked by telephone.

Over the next 90 years, nearly every household in North America and Europe acquired a phone. People took it for granted that they could pick up the phone and chat to friends at opposite ends of the country. When it came to international calls, there were often long delays—either because the line was crowded or because the signal took time to get through. Also, some countries did not have a cable link.

When the space age dawned in the 1960s, communications companies were quick to take advantage of the satellites being fired up into space. Telephone signals were translated into microwaves (like the rays in a microwave oven) and bounced around the world off satellites. Suddenly even the most out-of-the-way places could join the telephone network cheaply, and people could speak almost instantly to people across the far side of the world. Communications satellites not only transmit telephone messages instantly; they also handle TV and radio signals.

The telephone network was speeded up even further when fiber-optic cables began to be used in the 1970s. A laser or a light-emitting diode (LED) translates the electric signals of a telephone call into light impulses.

These are shone along a thin, transparent glass or plastic strand called an optical fiber. The light impulses are reflected off the internal surfaces of the fiber, and so they travel much faster and more cleanly than a conventional electric signal.

In the early 1980s several companies had begun to market cellular telephones, which used no wires at all. They sent and received messages via microwaves sent to special receiving stations. By the mid-1990s, a huge number of people used the compact mobile phones developed from these first bulky cell phones. The great revolution of the 1990s has been the Internet, which links computers all around the world using the telephone network.

▲ COMMUNICATIONS SATELLITE
Since the first communications satellite, called Telstar, was launched in 1962, satellites have dramatically accelerated the speed and ease with which all kinds of messages—from telephone conversations to TV broadcasts —can be beamed around the world.

▶ THE WORLD WIDE WEB
The World Wide Web is an amazingly clever way of finding your way around information on all the computers in the Internet. The information you can reach is set up as "sites" on all the millions of individual computers in the Net. The Web makes "hyperlinks" (fast links) to all the sites that contain the word you select. To find the right sites, you need a browser, which is a computer program that searches the entire Net.

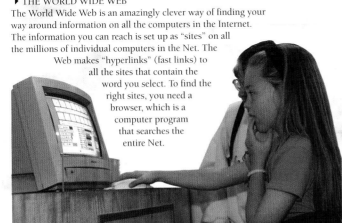

Key Dates

- 1844 Morse sends the first telegraph message.

- 1866 The first telegram is sent through the transatlantic cable.

- 1876 Bell sends the first telephone message.

- 1963 The first communications satellite is launched.

- 1960s The U.S. military develops ARPAnet to link computers.

- 1983 ARPAnet merges with university links to form the Internet.

- 1989 Tim Berners-Lee develops the World Wide Web.

The Moving Earth

▲ LYSTROSAURUS
*Finding fossils of
Lystrosaurus in Antarctica
was crucial evidence for the
theory that the continents
were once joined.
Lystrosaurus is a reptile
known to have lived in
China, Africa, and India 200
million years ago—and the
best explanation for finding
fossils in all four places is
that all four places were once
joined together.*

I
N RECENT YEARS geologists
have made the startling
discovery that the Earth's
surface is broken into 20 or
so giant slabs called
"tectonic plates." Even more
startling is the fact that these
plates are moving slowly
around the Earth. As they
move, the plates carry the
oceans and the continents
with them, so that they drift
around the world. This
discovery revolutionized our
understanding of the Earth's
surface, showing us why and
where earthquakes and
volcanoes occur and a great
deal more.

The idea that the continents
have moved is so astonishing that when a young
German meteorologist named Alfred Wegener
(1880–1930) first suggested it in 1923, he was
ridiculed. "Utter damn rot!" sneered the President of the
American Philosophical Society.

Yet it was not an altogether new idea. In the 17th
century the English thinker Francis Bacon had noticed
how strangely alike the coasts of South America and

◀ KOBE QUAKE
*The idea that tectonic
plates move has
transformed scientists'
understanding of how
earthquakes happen.
One day they may be
able to predict
earthquakes such as
the one that hit Kobe,
in Japan, in 1996.*

Africa are, and in the early 19th century a German
explorer had noticed remarkable similarities between
the rocks of Brazil and those of the African Congo. No
one thought much of this until naturalists found not
only identical turtles, snakes, and lizards in both South
America and Africa, but fossils of the ancient reptile
Mesosaurus in both Brazil and South Africa.

The accepted explanation was that the continents
had once been joined by necks of land that had since
vanished. The evidence was weak, but by the time
Wegener came up with his theory, the idea of land
bridges was firmly entrenched. Wegener's theory was
that all the continents had once been joined in a single
huge landmass which he called Pangaea, which had
split up hundreds of millions of years ago.

Only in the 1950s, when geologists began to explore
the ocean floor, did evidence in favor of Wegener start
to emerge. First, oceanographers found a great ridge

EARTHQUAKE AND VOLCANO ZONES
Soon after the idea of tectonic plates was
developed, geologists realized that the world's
major earthquake and volcano zones coincide with
the boundaries between the plates. It has now
become clear that most major earthquakes are
triggered by the immense forces generated as plates
grind together. When one plate drags past another,
the rock on each side of the boundary bends and
stretches a little way, then may snap suddenly. This
sudden rupture sends shock waves, called seismic
waves, shuddering through the ground, causing
earthquakes.

▶ MONITORING VOLCANOES
Most of the world's most explosive volcanoes occur in an
arc along the edge of what are called "convergent" plate
margins (places where two tectonic plates are coming
together). Volcanologists learn about volcanoes from
studying less-violent volcanoes away from plate margins
and above hot spots in the Earth's interior, such as this one.

◀ ERUPTING VOLCANO
Here you can actually see the molten lava exploding from the Earth's crust, where the pressure has become too great.

winding along the middle of the ocean floor through all the world's oceans, like a seam on a baseball. At the crest of this ridge was a deep central rift, or canyon.

In 1960 an American geologist, Harry Hess, stunned geologists by suggesting that the ocean floors might not be fixed, but were spreading rapidly from the mid-ocean ridge. As hot material wells up from the Earth's interior through the ridge's central rift, Hess suggested, it pushes the two halves of the ocean apart. Geologists were skeptical until, in the late 1960s, Frederick Vine and Drummond Matthews found stripes of strong and weak magnetism in the rocks on either side of the ridge. These stripes, they realized, must indicate ancient switches in the Earth's magnetic field, and so the stripes recorded the spreading of the ocean floor like the growth rings in a tree. A few years later, scientists on the research ship *Glomar Challenger* found that rocks got older the farther away from the ridge they were.

If Hess's theory that the ocean floor is spreading was right, then it seemed likely that Wegener's theory of continental drift was right too. In the 1980s geologists began to measure the distance between continents with astonishing accuracy, using laser beams bounced off satellites. They found that the continents really are moving, but the speed of this movement varies from place to place. North America and Europe are moving over 3/4 inch farther apart every year, which is faster than the rate at which a fingernail grows.

▼ KINDS OF VOLCANO
The movement of the plates creates different kinds of volcano. Where the plates are pulling apart—long the mid-ocean ridge, for instance—volcanoes ooze lava gently all the time, often bubbling up through the gap. The lava often flows out to form shallow shield volcanoes. Where the plates are pushing together, volcanoes are much more unpredictable and explosive— thick magma piles up steep, cone-shaped volcanoes.

shield volcano

cone volcano

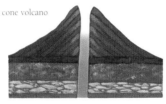
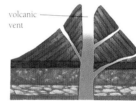

volcanic vent

▶ QUAKE WATCH
All around the world seismographic stations, such as the one shown here, are continually monitoring the earthquake vibrations generated as the Earth's tectonic plates grind together. The most violent earthquakes tend to occur in places where plates are sliding past each other—for example, along the San Andreas fault in California—or where one plate slides under another.

Key Dates

- 1923 Alfred Wegener suggests the idea of continental drift.

- 1956 Maurice Ewing, Bruce Heezen, and Marie Tharp discover the mid-ocean ridge.

- 1960 Harry Hess suggests that the ocean floors are spreading away from the mid-ocean ridge.

- 1963 Frederick Vine and Drummond Matthews find proof of ocean floor spreading in magnetic reversals in sea-bed rocks.

- 1967 Discovery of Lystrosaurus fossils in Antarctica.

- 1983 Satellites measure how fast tectonic plates are moving.

58

Artificial Materials

▲ ETHYLENE MOLECULE
Ethylene is a gas extracted from oil and natural gas. Ethylene molecules are made from four hydrogen atoms and two carbon atoms. Long chains of these molecules are put together to make polyethylene.

IN THE PAST, PEOPLE MADE things largely with natural materials such as wood and wool. During the 20th century, scientists developed an increasing range of synthetic, or manufactured, materials with properties that natural materials could not possibly match.

One of the biggest groups of synthetic materials is plastics, which are used in everything from spacecraft and car parts to bottles and artificial body parts. Plastics are incredibly light and can be molded into any shape. What gives plastic its special quality is the shape of its molecules (the smallest particles). With only a few exceptions, plastics are made from long organic (natural) molecules called polymers, which are made from lots of smaller molecules called monomers. Polyethylene, for instance, is a chain of 50,000 tiny molecules of an oil-extract called ethylene.

A few polymers, such as the tough fiber in plants known as cellulose, occur naturally. In the mid-1800s, scientists already knew that cellulose could be made into a brittle substance called cellulose nitrate. Then, in 1862, British chemist Alexander Parkes discovered

that by adding camphor he could make cellulose nitrate tough but bendy and easy to mold. The new material "Parkesine" never took off, but in 1869 American John Hyatt created a similar substance called celluloid. At first it was used simply to make billiard balls, but when Kodak started to make photographic film with it in 1889, its success was assured.

▼ RACING YACHT
To achieve lightness and strength, racing yachts are made from an increasing range of synthetic materials instead of the traditional wood and cotton. Typically the hull is a composite such as fiberglass or carbon-reinforced plastic, while the sails are made of a tough, light, completely waterproof nylon material.

POLYMER QUALITIES
Some polymers, such as the cellulose in wood and cotton, occur naturally, but most are now manufactured. They are all long chains of smaller molecules, altered slightly and repeated many times. In many polymers, the long molecules get tangled up like spaghetti, and it is the way they are tangled that gives a polymer its strength. If the strands are held tightly together, the result is a stiff plastic such as Lucite. If the strands slip over one another easily, it makes a bendy plastic such as polyethylene. Forcing the molecules through tiny holes lines them up to form a fiber such as nylon.

▶ LAVA LAMP
Plastics are easy to mold into almost any shape while warm, and once set, they hold their shape well. The clear cover for this lamp is molded plastic—typical of the fashion for molded plastic in the 1960s and 1970s.

◀ PVC
Polyvinyl chloride (PVC) is a synthetic polymer introduced in the 1920s. It can be either rigid or flexible. Rigid PVC is used for making objects such as bottles. Flexible PVC is used for making raincoats, garden hoses, and electrical insulation.

Since then, hundreds of plastics and other synthetic polymers have been developed, including Plexiglas, polyethylene, vinyl, cellophane, and a huge range of artificial fibers. The first of the synthetic fibers was nylon, which was created in the 1930s by Wallace Carothers, a chemist with the Du Pont company. In the 1920s, Carothers had found a way of making fibers out of very long polymer molecules stretched out in a machine called a molecular still. The stretching made the fibers strong and elastic, but they melted at very low temperatures. In 1935 he tried using a combination of chemicals called polyhexamethylene adipamide, which came to be called nylon.

Within a few years, Du Pont researchers had found a way of making the basic ingredients from petroleum, natural gas, and agricultural byproducts, and the first nylon products went on sale in 1939. People were so excited by this amazing new material that nylon mania swept the United States, and by the end of World War II everyone was wearing nylon-based clothes, and nylon stockings were a must for every woman. Nylon's

◀ RACING CYCLIST
Lightness really counts for a racing cyclist. This world-beating bike, instead of being made of metal like most bikes, is molded from carbon-reinforced plastic, which is far lighter than metal. Even the weight of the cyclist's clothes, shoes, and helmet is important. The synthetic fiber Lycra meets these requirements perfectly, in a way that no natural material can match.

toughness, elasticity, and moldability soon made it valued for furnishings, cars, and machinery as well as for clothes.

Since the introduction of nylon a whole new range of artificial fibers has been developed, including polyesters and Lycra, with a huge variety of uses. The big new area of polymer-based synthetic materials is "composites," which are made by combining two substances to obtain a material that has the qualities of both. Typically, one of the materials is a polymer. In carbon-reinforced plastic, tough carbon fibers are set within a polymer to make an amazingly strong but light material which is used to make anything from tennis rackets to racing car bodies. Kevlar, developed by Du Pont in 1971, is a composite based on nylon fibers set inside another polymer.

▼ PLASTIC DUCK
Plastics are so easily molded and so easy to make in bright colors that they have become very popular materials for making toys.

▲ BAKELITE
Bakelite was the first entirely synthetic plastic, invented by Leo Baekeland in 1909. It was made by treating phenol resin made from coal tar with formaldehyde. Like earlier plastics, it could be molded, but once molded, it set hard and was heatproof. Bakelite was also a good electrical insulator, so it was used for switches and plugs. It was also used to make radios, telephones, kitchenware, cameras, and much more.

Key Dates

- 1862 Alexander Parkes invents Parkesine, the first artificial polymer.
- 1869 John Hyatt invents celluloid.
- 1889 Kodak uses celluloid to make photographic film.
- 1909 Leo Baekeland invents Bakelite, the first entirely synthetic plastic.
- 1920 PVC is developed.
- 1935 Carothers develops nylon.
- 1939 Du Pont launches nylon.
- 1950s Carbon-fiber materials introduced.
- 1971 Kevlar created by Du Pont.

Life Changing

▲ G.M. TOMATOES
Many foods in our shops are already made with crops that have been genetically modified in some way. The genetically modified (G.M.) foods look no different from other foods.

During the 1950s, scientists discovered that all the instructions for life were carried in genetic code on the remarkable DNA molecule coiled inside every living cell. It took a while to crack the genetic code, but as they finally did, scientists began to realize that they might be able to manipulate it as a means of changing life's instructions.

In 1971, American microbiologists Daniel Nathans and Hamilton Smith discovered some chemicals called restriction enzymes. Restriction enzymes are like biological scissors, and they can be used to snip DNA in particular places. Other scientists soon found a biological glue—another enzyme, called DNA ligase, which can stick DNA back together. A few years later, American biochemist Paul Berg realized that by using restriction enzymes to cut DNA, and DNA ligase to glue it back together again, it would be possible to create entirely new and different DNA molecules. He called these new molecules "recombinant DNA." The remarkable thing about recombinant DNA was that it could be made to order, which made it completely different from anything that had ever existed before. This discovery was the beginning of what is now called genetic engineering. Scientists soon found, for example, that they could turn bacteria into protein factories by altering their genes. They simply extracted the DNA from the bacteria,

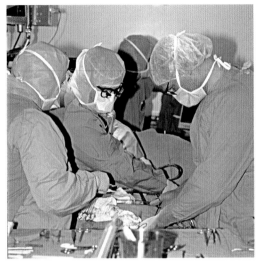

▲ HEART DISEASE
Many illnesses are inherited in the genes from parents; for example, a predisposition to heart disease can be inherited. One key area of genetic research focuses on ways of manipulating genes to cure genetic disorders such as these.

PERFECT REPLICAS
Usually each plant and animal has its own unique genes, which are different from those of every other plant and animal. You have a mix of genes from your mother, father, and grandparents, plus some that are your own and no one else's. "Cloning" means creating an organism (living thing) with exactly the same genes as another. The first clone was made when John Gurdon put the nucleus from a tadpole's gut cell, complete with DNA, into a frog's egg. The egg grew into a new tadpole, identical to the first.

Normally, new organisms grow from sex cells (from both parents) in which genes are mixed up. The DNA in each cell is a complete set of genes. Cloning uses the DNA from any body cell to grow a new creature. Since the new creature has the same genes, it is a perfect replica.

◀ DOLLY THE SHEEP
In 1997 Ian Wilmut and colleagues at Edinburgh's Roslin Institute made the first clone of an adult mammal. The clone was a sheep called Dolly. Scientists had thought adult mammals could not be cloned, but Dolly proved otherwise. Dolly grew from the nucleus of a cell taken from the teats of a Finn Dorset ewe and inserted in an egg in the womb of a Scottish Blackface ewe. The egg grew there to be born as a lamb with identical genes to the Finn Dorset ewe.

cut the right gene out of their DNA, inserted the one for the protein, and put it back in the bacteria. As the bacteria multiplied they would become a growing factory for the protein.

One valuable protein soon made like this was interferon. Interferons are proteins made by the human body which protect us against some viruses. However, the body makes only a tiny amount. By inserting doctored DNA into bacteria, it is possible to make lots of interferon reasonably cheaply. In the 1980s, scientists found how to use bacteria to make enzymes for detergents and melanin for suntan lotion, and also how to heighten the resistance of crops to pests and disease. Later, they discovered how to use sheep to produce insulin in their milk for diabetics. Scientists began to realize that there is no reason why, in future, we should not be able to transfer any gene from one living thing to another by using recombinant gene techniques. Soon they were investigating how to get bacteria and other living things to make certain substances, and many other things. Some scientists, for instance, began to work on how genetic disorders—illnesses inherited from your parents via your genes—might be cured. Others looked at how the genes of crops and farm animals might be modified to give them particular qualities. By adding to crops the genes from plants known to be distasteful or poisonous to crop pests, it might be possible to make crops pest resistant. The antifreeze genes from Antarctic fish, could be used to make other crops frost-resistant. However, as such experiments in the genetic modification of crops continued, they began to cause some public concern.

▶ G.M. CROPS
The idea of genetic modification of crops has become a topic of heated debate. Many scientists believe that genetic modification could dramatically boost crop production and reduce the need for pesticides. Others believe that the introduction of unnatural genes might have a devastating effect on natural ecosystems.

▼ IDENTICAL TWINS
Identical twins are the nearest nature provides to human clones. In theory, they both have identical genes because they grow from the same egg, which splits in two. In practice, however, many small differences appear as the twins develop inside their mother's womb.

Key Dates

- 1967 Gurdon creates the first clone, from a tadpole.

- 1970 Khorana creates the first truly artificial gene.

- 1971 Nathans and Smith discover restriction enzymes to snip DNA.

- 1973 Paul Berg discovers recombinant DNA techniques.

- 1973 Boyer uses recombinant DNA to create a chimera (combination of two species).

- 1975 Milstein produces the first monoclonal (single-cell clone) antibodies.

- 1997 Wilmut and colleagues clone Dolly the sheep, the first adult mammal clone.

62

Glossary

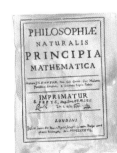

Brunel's *Great Eastern* steamship

A

anatomy The study of the structure of the body—where everything is and how it fits together.

antibiotic A drug typically based on a natural substance that attacks germs.

antiseptic Any substance that kills or inhibits germs.

aqueduct A manmade channel to supply water.

B

barometer A device for measuring air pressure.

Galileo's gravity experiment

C

capillary Microscopic blood vessel in the body, linking veins to arteries.

cathode-ray tube A special glass tube containing a vacuum. Inside, streams of electrons flow from a negative electrical terminal, or cathode.

chain reaction A nuclear fission reaction which gathers pace by itself. Neutrons split from each atom go on to split other atoms, and so split off more neutrons.

chimera A creature genetically engineered to include tissues from another creature.

chronometer Highly accurate clock used at sea to establish longitude.

clone A perfect genetic replica of a living thing, made from exactly the same genetic material.

combustion Burning.

compound A substance made by chemically combining two or more elements.

constellation One of the patterns of stars that astronomers use to find their way around the night sky. The pattern is entirely visual. There is no real connection between the stars in each constellation.

D

DNA Deoxyribonucleic acid, the basic chemical molecule inside every living cell which carries the genes—the cell's basic instructions for life and the instructions to make a new organism.

dynamo A device for generating electricity by rotating magnets past an electric coil.

E

electromagnetism The combined effects of electricity and magnetism.

element One of the 100 or so basic chemicals from which all others are built. None can be split into any other substance.

equinox One of the two days each year when night and day are equally long (12 hours) all over the world. One is on March 21, the other is on September 23.

evolution The gradual change of living species over time.

Newton's *Philosophiae naturalis principia mathematica*

PHILOSOPHIÆ
NATURALIS
PRINCIPIA
MATHEMATICA

IMPRIMATUR

LONDINI

G

galaxy A large cluster of stars.

gene A basic unit of hereditary material, instructing particular characteristics, such as eye color or hair type, to develop.

gravity The basic force of attraction between all matter which holds the Universe together.

I

immune system The body's natural defenses against disease.

induction The generation of electricity in a wire by a moving magnet.

internal combustion engine An engine that works by burning fuel inside a cylinder.

Internet The network linking millions of computers.

microchip

L

laser Light Amplification by Stimulated Emission of Radiation. A laser is a narrow beam of light of pure color that can be focused to give an incredibly intense beam or one that shines in a pinpoint over huge distances.

longitude Imaginary vertical lines circling the Earth from pole to pole. They tell navigators how far east or west they are of the prime meridian, a line of longitude running through Greenwich, England.

M

Map projection A system for showing a map of the curved surface of the Earth on flat paper.

N

nuclear fission
The release of nuclear energy by splitting the nuclei of large atoms such as uranium.

nuclear fusion
The release of nuclear energy by fusing together the nuclei of small atoms such as hydrogen.

Hubble telescope

P

phlogiston Material once thought to have been created during combustion.

physiology The study of body processes in cells, tissues, organs, and systems.

polygon A geometric shape with three or more straight sides.

polymer A compound made from a very long chain-like molecule.

pressure A pushing force. Air pressure is the force created by the combined assault of billions of fast-moving air molecules.

Q

quantum theory The idea that on a subatomic level, energy is always broken into tiny chunks, or quanta.

R

radiation The spread of energy as particles or waves, e.g. X-rays, light, or gamma rays.

radioactivity The gradual disintegration of large atoms, along with the emission of radiation.

T

tectonic plate One of the 20 or so giant slabs from which the Earth's surface is made.

transistor Tiny electronic switch which works automatically.

W

World Wide Web Computer system for linking computers together via the Internet.

Roman—viaduct

Index

A
alchemist 24, 25
America 10, 16, 34, 49, 57
anatomy 18-19, 29
antibiotics 44-5
aqueduct 14, 15
archaeology 39
Archimedes 12-13
Aristotle 22
arithmetic 8, 9
Asia 10, 16, 50
astronomy 10–11, 18, 20–1, 40, 42–3
atom 24, 25, 39, 46–7

B
Babylonia 8, 9, 10
barometer 22
Bell, Alexander Graham 29, 54
Big Bang 42–3
biochemistry 48–9
biologist 60
botany 30, 31
bouyancy 12–13
Boyle 22, 24, 25
bridge 14, 15
Britain 26–7, 30, 31, 36, 37, 45, 50
Brunel, 31, 62

C
canal 26
car 34–5
caravel 16, 64
Catholicism 21
CD 50
central heating 14
chemistry 24–25, 28, 45, 59, 60
China 9, 16, 36, 56
chronometer 16
clock 16
cloning 60–1
Cold War 52
Columbus 10, 16
communications 54–5
compass 16, 17, 29
computer 38, 45, 49, 50–1, 54, 55
Copernicus 11, 20, 21, 42
Curie, Marie and Pierre 39
cyberspace 45

D
da Gama, Vasco 16
Darwin, Charles 32–3
da Vinci, Leonardo 18, 36
Democritus 24
Dias, Bartolomeu 16
dinosaur 32, 43
disease 44–5, 60, 61
DNA 48–9, 60–1
dynamo 28, 64

E
Earth 11, 18, 20–1, 31, 43, 52, 56–7
ecosystem 61
Egypt 9, 10, 11, 12, 18, 30
Einstein, Albert 40–1, 46
electricity 28–9, 38, 50, 58, 59
electronics 17, 50–1
element 24, 25
energy 28, 40, 46–7
engineering 9, 14–15
Euclid 8, 9
Eudoxus 8
Europe 16, 26, 32, 53, 55, 57
evolution 30–1

F
factory 26–7, 30
Faraday, Michael 28, 29
farming 10, 26, 61
flying 36–7
force 13, 22–3, 28
France 15, 30, 36, 37, 39, 50
Franklin, Benjamin 28

G
Galen 18
Galileo 13, 20, 21, 22, 23, 24, 40
genes 49, 60–1
geography 10
geology 33, 56–7
geometry 8, 9, 12
Germany 35, 37, 44, 47
gravity 13, 22, 23
Greece 8, 9, 10, 12, 14, 20, 22, 24, 28, 30, 36–7
Greenwich 17

H
Harvey, William 19
Henry, Joseph 28, 29
Hipparchus 10
Hubble 42, 43
Huygens 16, 22

I
India 16, 56
Industrial Revolution 26–7, 30
Internet 29, 54–5
iron 12, 26, 27
irrigation 12
Italy 12, 13, 14, 15, 18, 19, 21, 29, 47

J
Japan 47, 56

L
latitude 16, 17
Lavoisier, Antoine 24, 25
Leeuwenhoek 18, 22
Leibnitz 22
lever 13
light 38–9, 40, 41
longitude 16, 17

M
machine 12, 26–7, 28, 30, 37, 50
Magellan, Ferdinand 16
magnetism 28–9, 38, 57
Malphigi, Marcello 18, 19
map 10, 16–17, 21
mathematics 8–9, 12, 13, 30
matter 24–5, 58–9
medicine 18, 44–5
Mercator, Gerhardus 17
microchip 50–1
microscope 18, 19, 49
Middle Ages 16, 24, 36
Middle East 8, 12
Mongol Empire 16
motion 22–3, 40–1

N
navigation 16–17
Netherlands, the 17, 18, 20, 40
Newton 22, 23, 24, 38
nuclear power 46–7, 54

O
oceanography 57

P
Pasteur, Louis 44, 45
Persian Empire 10
philosopher 12, 22, 24, 25
physician 18, 19
physiology 19
planets 11, 20–1, 22, 23
Portugal 16
power 27, 30–1, 34, 46–7
prehistoric 10
Priestley, Joseph 24, 25
Ptolemy 10, 11, 20
Pyramid 9, 10
Pythagoras 8

R
radiation 38–9
railroads 30–1
religion 11
Renaissance 18, 19
roads 14, 15, 34–5
Rome 12, 14–15, 18, 21
Russia 25

S
satellite 52, 55, 57
scientist 12–13, 20, 22, 23, 24, 28, 31, 38, 40, 41, 44, 45, 46, 47, 51, 56, 58, 61
ship 12–13, 16–17, 30–1, 40, 58
Soviet Union 52, 53
space 40–1, 51, 52–3, 55
Stonehenge 10
surgery 19
synthetic materials 58–9

T
telegraph 54
telephone 29, 54, 55, 59
telescope 21, 42, 43
television 28, 38, 39, 51, 55
time 40–1
trade 26
transistor 50, 51

U
United States 29, 31, 47, 52, 53, 54
Universe 11, 20, 21, 22, 23, 28, 42–3

V
vaccination 44
Vesalius 19
virtual reality 51
Vitruvius 14
Volta, Alessandro 28, 29

W
World War 1 36
World War 2 17, 47, 50
World Wide Web 54, 55

dynamo

caravel

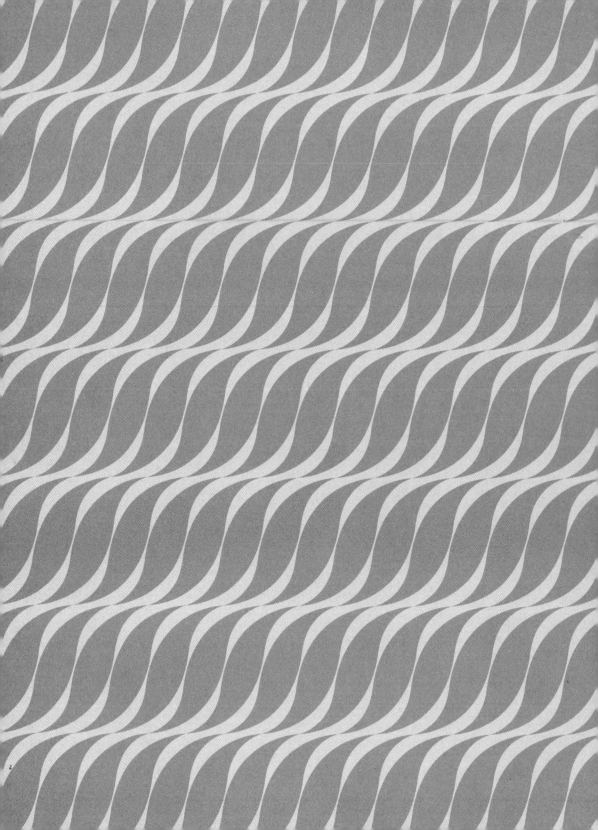